"This book offers a straightforward approach to building communication skills with your teenager. It addresses one of the most challenging areas of parenting teens with simple, easy-to-follow language and ideas that will help you create an environment where communication happens naturally in your home."

DOUG FIELDS, PASTOR TO STUDENTS
SADDLEBACK CHURCH

"Teens will talk to their parents if they know their parents will listen and understand. This delightful book provides everything a parent needs to do both really well. Definitely one of the best parenting books I've ever read on understanding and communicating with teenagers."

WAYNE RICE, DIRECTOR
UNDERSTANDING YOUR TEENAGER

"Prayer, communication, and discipleship are the three bridges parents must build if they want to ignite a passion for Christ in their kids. Kent and Connie give you all the tools you need to build the communication bridge."

BARRY ST. CLAIR, PRESIDENT
REACH OUT YOUTH SOLUTIONS

How to Get Your Teen to Talk to You is a great resource filled not only with practical wisdom, but also with helpful insights into parent/teen communication. With three daughters of my own, two of whom are teens, I enjoyed every moment of this book and recommend it highly to strengthen your communication and overall relationship with your teens."

DANN SPADER, EXECUTIVE DIRECTOR
SONLIFE MINISTRIES

"This book has fifty-two incredibly practical lessons on developing a better relationship with your teenager. It is practical, challenging, affirming—a must-read for every parent!"

JIM BURNS, PH.D., PRE
YOUTHBUILDER!

"Researchers know there's nothing more important to teenagers' faith development than conversations about faith with their moms and dads. That's why this book meets such a crucial need, and meets it well. Busy parents who are desperate for real ideas for opening up conversation with their teenagers—not just another list of supposed-to's—will find them here. Read this book, try its ideas, and your relationship with your teenager will improve."

RICK LAWRENCE, EXECUTIVE EDITOR
GROUP MAGAZINE

"How to Get Your Teen to Talk to You is a home run in the game of parent/teen relations! A delightful scrapbook of "teenage journey," it is also a first-rate primer on effective communication. Kent Julian and Connie Grigsby offer keen insights, frank advice, and practical helps on caring, connecting, and communicating with teens. Their book should be required reading for parents or grandparents—and anyone who wants to improve their ministry to teens."

DR. PETER NANFELT, PRESIDENT
CHRISTIAN AND MISSIONARY ALLIANCE

HOW to get your Teen to talk to you

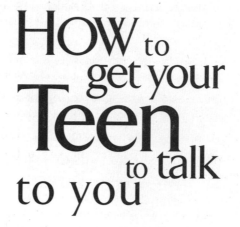

Connie Grigsby and Kent Julian

Multnomah® Publishers *Sisters, Oregon*

HOW TO GET YOUR TEEN TO TALK TO YOU
published by Multnomah Publishers, Inc.

© 2002 by Connie Grigsby and Kent Julian

International Standard Book Number: 1-59052-064-5

Cover image by Getty Images/Tim Macpherson

For ease of reading and to be inclusive, the authors
have alternated between male and female pronouns.

Unless otherwise indicated, Scripture quotations are from:
The Holy Bible, New International Version © 1973, 1984 by International Bible
Society, used by permission of Zondervan Publishing House

Multnomah is a trademark of Multnomah Publishers, Inc.,
and is registered in the U.S. Patent and Trademark Office.

The colophon is a trademark of Multnomah Publishers, Inc.

Printed in the United States of America

For information:
MULTNOMAH PUBLISHERS, INC.
POST OFFICE BOX 1720
SISTERS, OREGON 97759

Library of Congress Cataloging-in-Publication Data
Grigsby, Connie.
    How to get your teen to talk to you / by Connie Grigsby and Kent Julian.
        p. cm.
Includes bibliographical references.
    ISBN 1-59052-064-5 (pbk.)
    1. Parent and teenager--Religious aspects--Christianity. 2. Interpersonal
communication--Religious aspects--Christianity. 3. Child rearing--Religious apsects--
Christianity. 4. Christian teenagers--Religious life. I. Julian, Kent. II. Title.
    BV4529 G745 2003
    248.8'45--dc21   2002151014

03 04 05 06 07 08—10 9 8 7 6 5 4 3 2 1 0

To my three teenage daughters—
Cassidy Marie,
Whittney Brooks, and
Maddison Sinclaire.

You put the sparkle in my days!
Thanks for talking to me.
Thanks even more for loving me.
You, along with your dad, make the journey more delightful.
I thank God for each of you.
I'll love you forever....
—Mom

To Kathy—
My best friend and soul mate.
You are absolutely incredible,
and I'm the luckiest man on earth!

To Mom and Dad—
I wouldn't trade my teenage years with you for anything.
So much of who you are is in this book.
Thank you!

To Grandma and Grandpa—
I owe my heritage to you.
You are heroes in my life.
—Kent

TABLE OF CONTENTS

ACKNOWLEDGMENTS 11
INTRODUCTION—A Scrapbook of the Journey 13

I. THE ART OF BEING
Authentic Character Counts!

1. Help Wanted: Parent of Teen 19
   A Parental Job Description

2. Ain't Nothing like the Real Thing, Baby! 22
   Authenticity Is Huge

3. The Influence Ladder 24
   *Why Peers Influence Our Teens So Much, and
   What You Can Do About It*

4. For Better or for Worse 27
   The Importance of Loving Your Spouse

5. Wake Up on the Right Side of the Bed 30
   A Personal Check on Beginning Your Days Right

6. More than Food and Clothing 33
   Is Your Teen's Heart and Soul Well Dressed?

7. A Promise Is a Promise 36
   Can Your Teen Trust Your Word?

8. Simplify Your Life 38
   Are You Too Busy or Too Stressed to Talk?

9. Listening Right 41
   How to Make Your Teen Feel Heard

10. Listening Wrong 45
    How to Make Your Teen Feel Unheard

II. WHY IS OUR ANGEL ACTING LIKE A PRIMATE?
A Sneak Peek at Today's Teenager and the Youth Culture

11. Developmentally Speaking 51
    Helping Your Teen Navigate the Chaos

12. I Want to Be Me 55

The Importance of Individuality and Autonomy

13. Technologically Advanced, Media Numbed 59
    Facing the Giants of Youth Culture

14. Prevent Defense 62
    Teenagers and Substance Abuse

15. Decoding Postmodernism 66
    Looking through the Postmodern Lens

III. LINGUISTIC LESSONS
Learning to Talk with (Not at) Your Teen

16. Choose Your Battles Wisely 73
    Or You'll Be Fighting All the Time

17. If You're Open, I'm Open 76
    Are You Available?

18. To Spoil or Not to Spoil 79
    Can't Buy Me Love

19. Saying No and Meaning It 83
    How to Say No Correctly

20. Say Yes as Often as Possible 86
    The Deaf-Ear Antidote

21. The Myth of Quality Time 89
    Wake up and Smell the Coffee!

22. Say It and Spray It 92
    Know Your Teen's Love Language

23. Get a Life! 96
    Is Your Teen Claustrophobic?

24. Play Fair 98
    What Not to Say

25. Changing the Rules 101
    How to Ask Questions That Get Responses

26. Anger 104
    Yours and Theirs

27. Acceptance 108
    The Lap of Luxury

IV. BECOMING BILINGUAL
Learning to Speak "Teenager"

28. Why Teens Don't Raise Their Hands Anymore 113
    The Communication Rules Have Changed

29. Blastoff and Reentry 116
    Making Mornings and Evenings Count

30. The Fun of Fun 119
    Laughter Is a Great Medicine

31. Huggie Sandwiches 122
    Buffering the Negative with the Positive

32. Family Meetings 125
    Finding Time to Talk

33. Peer Fear 128
    Helping Teens Face Peer Pressure

V. NOW WE'RE TALKING!
Moving from Communication to Connection

34. Bury the Cold Treatment 135
    A Conversational Warm-Up

35. Serve Together 139
    Growing Closer

36. Can Parents Be Friends? 142
    The Issue of Friendship

37. Discover Their Passions 145
    What Makes Their Hearts Beat Faster?

38. Open House 148
    Making Your Home Teen-Friendly

39. Do You Promise Not to Tell? 151
    The Importance of Confidentiality

VI. A LITTLE SEX TALK
Talking with Your Teen about the Guy/Girl Thing

40. Anatomy 101 157
    Beating the System to Talking about the Body and Sex

41. And They Call It...Puppy Love 160
    Teenage Love and Romance

42. Good Sex 162
    Is There Such a Thing?

43. For Guys Only 167
    The Big M

44. For Girls Only 171
    Questions, Questions, Questions

45. Navigating the Dating Maze 175
    When Is It Okay to Date?

VII. AFTER ALL IS SAID, BUT NOT DONE
A Few Extra Helpful Tips

46. Personality Plus 181
    Customizing Your Approach

47. Two! Four! Six! Eight! 184
    Practicing the Art of Encouragement

48. Seize the Moment 187
    See Life through Their Eyes

49. Praise!   190
    Catch Your Teen Doing Something Good

50. Admit Your Mistakes 193
    The Importance of Asking for Forgiveness

51. Now I Lay Me Down to Sleep 196
    Making Prayer a Priority

52. Letting Go 199
    Working Yourself out of a Job

EPILOGUE—It's Never Too Late to Start 203

STATEMENT PAGE—What We Believe 207

APPENDIX—Suggested Resources 209

NOTES 211

ACKNOWLEDGMENTS

Thank you to Renee DeLoriea, our editor and friend, for having a vision and excitement about this book that equaled our own. You melded our two voices into one and infused us with fresh clarity and purpose—time and again. We especially admire your desire to honor God in all you do. We appreciate this more than we can say.

Thank you to Bill Jensen for trusting me (Connie) enough to bring a first-time author on board. May your trust be found worthy.

Thank you to Nancy Thompson, from whose mind the idea for this book first came. You are a dear friend and a tremendous encourager.

Thank you to the many young voices who allowed their words to be heard at the beginning of every chapter and throughout the book as well. A special thanks to the students and parents from Christ Community Church and Central Gwinnett Alliance Church for generously sharing your thoughts and hearts. Each of you is special indeed!

Thank you to our families and friends, who prayed us through this book and cheered us on along the way.

Thank you to Jim Vitti, Diane Jelkin, and Gerri Shope for encouraging a couple of wanna-be writers to write! Several years ago each of you saw something in us that we didn't see in ourselves—thank you!

Thank you to Kathy and Wes, our spouses, for helping this book take shape. Your thoughts and ideas were invaluable. Kathy, we'll give you a reference for proofing and editing anytime you need one, and, Wes, thanks for covering so many bases, including offering insight and counsel when asked.

Thank you to Multnomah Publishers for partnering with us and for investing in the kingdom in so many ways. We count it a blessing to be a part of your family.

Most of all, thanks be to God. We're forever grateful.

INTRODUCTION

A Scrapbook of the Journey

Do you enjoy scrapbooks? Some people absolutely love them, spending hours clipping and pasting. But all the photos, calligraphy, and pressed flowers aren't what make scrapbooks special. Instead, the memories—jarred by the memorabilia—are what give significance to these journals. Indeed, scrapbooks simply call to remembrance the journey we call life.

If you were to fashion a scrapbook, what recollections would fill your pages? Good ones? Painful ones? Indifferent ones?

Your teenager is on a journey too. With each passing moment, memories and building blocks are being added to his repertoire. Surely one of your heart's greatest desires is that this scrapbook will overflow with wonderful recollections of the past that provide solid building blocks for the future.

WHY THIS BOOK?

As we all know, one-sided communication isn't very effective. Yet this is how many parent/teen conversations go: the parent talking (or lecturing) while the teen listens (or endures). But because this book primarily concentrates on *how to get your teen talking with you* rather than on *how to talk to (or at) your teen,* it cuts right to the heart of the matter. In essence, this book serves as a catalyst to genuine, authentic communication between you and your teenager.

Why take this approach? Simple. If you know how to talk to your teen, but she's not listening, what good is that? However, if your teen talks with you in a genuine way, you know authentic, two-way communication is taking place (as long as you return the favor)!

So this book is designed specifically to help you get your teen talking with you. Through this book, we *aim* to:

- Help you gain greater appreciation for what's happening in your teen's life. Why? Because teenagers are much more willing to talk with us when they know we understand.

- Affirm you in your role as parent. Why? Because you're the most important person in your teen's life—regardless of whether she admits it.
- Equip you with practical parenting skills. Why? Because parenting teenagers is a different "animal" than parenting younger children, and many of today's parents don't make this transition smoothly.
- Encourage you to hang in there. Why? Because "throwing in the towel" would be counterproductive.

On the other hand, this book is not:

- A crash course on parenting. *It won't teach you everything you need to know in ten easy steps.*
- A crisis-intervention tool. *Instead, it focuses on "normal" adolescents (is there such a thing?) and how to get them talking.*

We (the authors) have known each other for almost a decade. Our paths originally crossed when Connie's daughters were involved in Kent's youth ministry. Later, Wes and Connie volunteered in the ministry and grew to appreciate Kent's love for God, parents, and teens.

Kent and Kathy have rubbed shoulders with thousands of parents during their years in ministry. In order to glean insight for their own parenting, they've always kept an eye out for parents who raise great kids. As Kent likes to say, "Wes and Connie always made our top-ten list."

OUR CONNECTION

Throughout the years, we have shared many conversations about our passion for parent/teen communication. Interestingly, this passion evolved from different perspectives: Connie as a parent of teenagers, and Kent as a youth pastor. Connie's heart broke each time she saw parents and their teens at odds with one another, while Kent felt like his attempts to help students were near futile if they refused to talk with their parents.

We both knew that rich, healthy parent/teen communication was possible (we'd seen it, for goodness sake), but we just didn't see it happening very often—even in families that considered it a high priority. Time and again we saw that getting teens to open up and getting parents to really hear what is being said are necessary elements for unlocking that authentic, two-way conversation every parent hopes for. Hence, the book *How to Get Your Teen to Talk to You* was born.

BEFORE WE BEGIN

Before opening this scrapbook, here are a few thoughts that will help you get the most out of our adventure together.

First, not every chapter in this book directly addresses the issue of getting teens to talk. Many chapters tackle this subject head-on. However, to give you other essential pieces to the puzzle, we've added chapters describing ways to create an environment that encourages meaningful conversations.

Second, while this book is an easy read, it's not a shallow read. Therefore, stop and reflect regularly. Even more, allow the words to steer you into intentional action. Since the book is divided into fifty-two chapters, consider reading one per week. Record your thoughts in a journal, and add the new principles to your communication toolbox. Hopefully in just a short while, your relationship with your teen will be enriched in a multitude of ways.

Third, keep in mind that this is not a comprehensive study of parent-teen relationships. In fact, you will find that we do not address some of the grittier complexities that sometimes arise. For resources that wrestle with these issues, check out the appendix.

Finally, in no way do we write as experts who have arrived. Like you, we are fellow travelers. We feel compelled to share this information with you because we've seen many parents break through the roadblocks that were hindering their teens from talking to them. Our desire is to help you develop inexhaustible communication with your teen that will bear fruit for a lifetime.

So open this scrapbook that will encourage your teen to talk to you and help you understand what he's saying! When this occurs, you'll find that your love and respect for one another will be rooted more firmly than ever before, paving the way for a lifetime of precious memories!

ABOUT THE AUTHORS

Connie Grigsby is the coauthor of *How to Get Your Husband to Talk to You* and *The Politically Incorrect Wife* (formerly titled *Is There a Moose in Your Marriage?*), a finalist for the literary Gold Medallion Award. A popular teacher and speaker, she has a heart for helping others discover life's bottom line. She and her husband, Wesley, are the parents of three teenagers.

Kent Julian is a veteran youth pastor currently serving over two thousand churches as the National Director of Alliance Youth. He loves seeing teenagers realize their potential and believes parents are *the* key to making this happen. He and his wife, Kathy, are the parents of three children.

THE ART OF BEING
Authentic Character Counts!

❧

What we believe is evidenced by how we live, not just by what we say. And since our *doing* comes out of our *being*, how we live on the outside ends up only being a reflection of who we are on the inside.

Do we want our teens to talk to us? Then nothing is more important than the strength of our own integrity, faith, and character. If our teens trust and respect us—and feel secure in our unconditional love—they will talk to us. Authentic character counts!

CHAPTER ONE

HELP WANTED: PARENT OF TEEN

A Parental Job Description

*The trouble with being a parent is
that by the time you're experienced…you're unemployed.*
ANONYMOUS

❧

The job description of a parent is to provide a secure environment that champions solid standards.

Obviously, every kid at every age needs this. But with teens, such an environment provides fertile ground for them to respect and trust us, look to us for guidance, and talk more honestly and openly with us.

So what does this haven of rest—with unconditional love as its foundation—look like?

STANDARDS

This safe haven is framed with standards—the plumb line by which life is measured and the starting point for discerning right from wrong. These standards provide the structure for everyday life. And in many ways, they determine the very quality of life.

Do you ever wonder which standards you should champion? With the glut of belief systems today, how do you know which standards are best? Because the Bible is the ultimate and perfect source of standards, let God's Word be your guide.

Parents' actions speak volumes about their own standards. Because how we live—not what we say—is the clearest reflection of what we believe. When we reflect strength of character and love to our children, we pass along those standards to them. And then, when they are no longer living under our roof, those standards will be their North Star…pointing to abundant life.

SECURITY

The solid standards mentioned above can only be developed in a secure and loving environment. Teenagers need a safe and loving place where they can develop their own beliefs, values, and identities.

Are you providing this kind of environment? Does your teen feel safe enough to discuss anything and everything with you?

As a youth pastor, I (Kent) spend a lot of time talking to teenagers. Since recently moving back to Atlanta after several years, I have reconnected with some of the guys, now in their late twenties, who were in my first youth group fifteen years ago. One guy, whom I'll call Jay, always had a great relationship with his mom and dad. When we recently met for coffee to catch up on old times, I asked him how his parents were doing. He proceeded to go off for ten minutes, telling me how great they were and how much he respected them. As I dug deeper, I asked him what made his parents so great. He replied without hesitation, "I've always been able to talk to them about anything. They love me unconditionally."

As Jay grabbed at the chance to talk about the secure environment his parents had created for him, I couldn't help but think of a very different story—about a very different family. A few weeks earlier I had done some catching up with another guy named Blake. As we sipped our coffee (yes, I love coffee), he asked my advice on a number of issues. When I asked him what his parents' take was on these things, he said, "We don't talk about stuff like this. My family is detached relationally."

Amazing! Here was a young man, almost thirty years old, who still didn't feel safe enough with his parents to discuss issues that were very important to him.

Like we said…security is a big deal.

Safety

You've probably heard the saying, "You can fool some of the people some of the time, but you can't fool all of the people all of the time." But when it comes to relating to teens, we would have to say: "You can't fool any of them ever!"

Yes, when it comes to character, teens have a sixth sense. They can smell a fake a mile away. If we don't live what we say we believe, they'll see right through us. Even more, they'll never confide in us because they don't feel they can trust us to safely guide them in the right way. But, if they can trust us to point them in the right direction, down a path we are already on ourselves, they will look to us for guidance.

❧

Bottom Line: Teens talk more honestly and openly in a secure home environment where solid standards are championed.

CHAPTER TWO

AIN'T NOTHING LIKE THE REAL THING, BABY!

Authenticity Is Huge

Actions speak louder than words, especially for parents and pastors.
JENNA, 15

❧

In May of 1990, my (Connie) dad had quintuple bypass surgery. My youngest daughter and I flew to Oklahoma to be with my parents while my husband and twins stayed back at our home in Omaha. For the next week we became extremely familiar with the hospital. In fact, when my cousin Jeanette asked my not quite two-year-old daughter where her new home was, she replied, "The hospital."

Since visiting hours were limited, we had a lot of time on our hands and would often visit the hospital gift shop. On one such visit, a plaque on the wall caught my attention.

Small and simply framed were these poignant words:

> *Your walk talks*
> > *And your talk talks*
> *But your walk talks more*
> > *Than your talk talks.*

As we briefly mentioned earlier, teens are geniuses at zeroing in on hypocritical behavior. If we want our teens to talk to us and—far more than that—if we want our teens to respect us, we need to make certain our walk and our talk line up.

For instance, let's say Johnny just turned thirteen. As he and his dad walk toward the ticket booth at the movie theater, they both look at the large sign indicating ticket prices are five dollars for children, ages three to twelve; and ten dollars for adults, ages thirteen and older. Dad and son look at each other and give the signal—they've done this before. Johnny is thirteen, not twelve, but Dad buys him a child-priced ticket anyway—both know they'll spend the "saved" money on concessions. Of course, the ticket agent doesn't question the dad because he doesn't look like someone who would lie.

Dad may have thought he saved five dollars, and Johnny may be happy with his extra large popcorn and soda. But something of much greater value than a measly five dollars is at stake here: Johnny knows he's thirteen. Dad's probably told him that lying and stealing are wrong, but this little lesson in lying, cheating, and stealing says just the opposite.

Johnny may not know what the word *integrity* means, but in his gut he knows that the deception was wrong…and he knows his dad knows it too.

There really isn't any such thing as a little white lie. Involving children in lying, cheating, and stealing is always a very big thing. And yet many parents don't even think twice about telling their children to tell a caller that they're not home—when they are! Or telling them to tell their teachers they were sick—when in fact you extended your family vacation.

On the one hand, we ask our kids to tell lies when it's convenient for *us,* but then on that same day we ground them for lying to us when it's convenient for *them.*

Talk about mixed messages! No wonder they don't bother talking to us.

So this brings us to the question: *Who wants to talk over the issues of life with a thief and a liar?* Not anyone we know. Sure, our kids may still talk to us, but it won't be about anything of much depth or significance.

Even if we are honest most of the time, our kids will still notice the couple of times we shade the truth to our own advantage…and they will wonder why we preach one message but live a different one.

Kids are smart. *If we can't be trusted to be honest with a five dollar difference in the price of a ticket, why should they trust us with what is near and dear to their teenage souls?*

❧

Bottom Line: Your character shouldn't be "for sale."

CHAPTER THREE

THE INFLUENCE LADDER

Why Peers Influence Our Teens So Much, and What You Can Do about It

If you were going to guess how a kid is going to turn out, one of the first things you'd do is look at who's influencing his life.
WHITTNEY, 18

Over the years, I've (Kent) sat with literally dozens of parents as they've poured out their hearts to me about the negative influence peers have on their teen.

- "Katie's a good girl, but her friends drag her down."
- "We don't understand why Eric got into drugs, but we know his new friends had something to do with it."
- "Trish has such an attitude, and it all started when she began hanging out with Jenny."

Can you identify with these statements?

When parents came to me with concerns like these, my counsel, I hate to admit, was rather lame. I'd usually say something like: "We both know that good kids can be influenced by bad ones. What's more, there's not much we can do about it because we no longer sit on the top rung of the influence ladder. Peers have stolen that position. Our best hope is to somehow hold on to the second, third, or fourth rung and lovingly wait out the turbulent years. Therefore, try all you can to influence your teen, even if she doesn't respond. With a little luck and a ton of prayer, perhaps your teen will make it through these years and realize all the advice you gave was pretty accurate. In fact, I was a lot like your kid. And you know what? Once I reached my early twenties, I realized my parents weren't so dumb after all. I even went back and told them I discovered how right they'd been."

I know! I know! Most parents probably didn't leave with a whole lot of hope, but what else could I do?

Imagine my surprise then when I discovered that according to most studies and research, parents are the most influential people in a teen's life! Was this information for real, or was it simply archaic writings gathered during the "Leave It to Beaver" era?

Further exploration confirmed this information as authentic. In fact, it was even more amazing than I had imagined. For instance, Wayne Rice and David Veerman, in their book *Understanding Your Teenager,* cite the following studies:

- In 1997, researchers at the University of Minnesota and the University of North Carolina surveyed twelve thousand students in grades seven through twelve and found that the closer teenagers were to their parents, the less likely they were to smoke, use drugs, drink alcohol, engage in violence, commit suicide, or have sex at a young age. They also discovered that a teenager's connection with school and teachers played a significant role.

- A survey of 272,400 teenagers found that 70 percent of teens identified their parents as the most important influence in their lives. Only 21 percent say the same thing about peers, and just 8 percent pointed to the media.[1]

Other studies could be cited, but the point is clear. Parents, not peers, are the most influential people in the lives of teenagers. In fact, according to many researchers, the statistics of who has the most influence on teenagers flesh out like this:

1. Parents
2. Extended family
3. Adults outside the home—coaches, youth workers, teachers, and friends of parents.
4. Peers
5. Media—TV, movies, and music

This list, of course, contradicts the commonly held view that peers are the most influential people in the lives of our teens. So why do we assume that this "peer myth" is accurate? Wayne Rice and David Veerman suggest that "it's because for a growing segment of the teen population, it *is* true."[2] In fact, peers have such an enormous influence on so many teens today because the top three influential groups—parents, extended family, and caring adults—are absent. In summation, peer influence wins out when parents are too busy, when extended family moves away, and when there is no connection with adult role models. It's influence by default!

Think about it; it makes perfect sense. Teens gravitate toward being influenced by the oldest person who cares, respects, encourages, and positively challenges them. Consider your own life: Who was the most influential person during your teen years? For me, it was my parents, grandparents, Dan Glaze, Steve Morgan, and Jim Vaught—all relatives or adult role models. Each one impacted me big-time! Looking back, I realize that I connected with them for the very reason spelled out above. They cared for me, respected me, encouraged me, and positively challenged me. In fact, I didn't just like them; I was drawn to them. Not surprisingly, they ended up being my most cherished advisors and counselors.

So here are a few questions for you: Are peers on the top rung of your teen's influence ladder? Are they there by default? If your answers are yes, what steps can you take to move back up the ladder? Even more, what can you do to position coaches, teachers, and church members you respect higher up on the ladder as well? If you start climbing today, you can take back what is rightfully yours—the top rung of the influence ladder.

∽

Bottom Line: Start climbing by caring, respecting, encouraging, and challenging your teen!

CHAPTER FOUR

FOR BETTER OR FOR WORSE

The Importance of Loving Your Spouse

My dad once told me that while he loved us kids to death, no one could take the place of our mother. That made me feel great!

MADDI, 13

⤌⤍

What page in your teens' scrapbook would you most like to change? If you are like most parents, you would probably wish you could edit the page titled "Marriage." This is certainly true for me (Connie).

I still remember the many times we were sitting around the dinner table and our twins would ask, "How come you two never talk? Never hug? Never go out on a date together? How come…? How come…? How come…?"

They had every reason to ask. Why? Because Wes had grown distant, I'd grown cold, and our marriage had grown stale.

During that time one of the girls made a statement that summed up the tainted image of marriage we conveyed. We were at a restaurant and noticed a couple seated nearby who were having a wonderful time together.

"I wonder if they're married," Wes mused.

"No, Daddy," Cassidy said.

"How can you tell?" Wes asked.

"Because they're having fun together," our then nine-year-old daughter replied innocently. "Only couples who are dating have fun. When you get married, you don't have fun anymore."

Excuse me for a moment while I wipe this tear from my eye and swallow this lump in my throat. Although those years have since faded, the unhappy memories still bring me sadness.

Your kids are watching you too. What model of marriage are you portraying to them?

This is an important question for parents to ask—and ask often—because children's sense of what is *normal* is derived primarily from what they see in their parents' marriage. Every day they see dozens of images of you and your spouse—how you communicate, how you show love to one another, how you deal with conflict—and they'll carry these images into adulthood and into their own marriages. With this in mind, it's easy to see how loving your spouse is one of the greatest gifts you can give to your children.

You can't change another's behavior, but you can change your own.

Ideally, your teen will see two parents loving each other deeply. But even if he can't see a two-way exchange of love, you still can choose to love your spouse and exhibit unconditional love in action.

Don't allow your feelings to dictate your behavior, which is easier said than done! Feelings have a way of catching up to thoughtful, intentional actions. Remember, sometimes you have to act now and feel later.

You may be asking, "But where do I begin?" Great question! Just by asking that, you are well on your way to warming your home.

We recommend that you try some of these "jump starts":

- Think positive, not negative, thoughts about your mate.
- Give your spouse the benefit of the doubt; overlook quirks.
- Surprise your spouse with an unexpected act of kindness.
- Speak positively to others about your spouse. How you see your spouse greatly affects how your child sees this person, too.
- Pray for your spouse. Ask God to love your mate through you.
- Reintroduce pet names: Darling! Sweetheart!
- Soften your look. So often, parents look at their children softly but look at one another with disinterest or even disdain.
- Show respect. We asked kids what they would most like to change about their parents. One of their top answers: "That they'd treat each other better."

Also ask yourself, "Who ranks highest on my list of priorities—

my kids or my spouse?" If you're like most parents today, your children rank higher; but when priorities are upside down like this, teens are negatively affected. As John Rosemond says:

> By putting children first in your family, you guarantee they will become manipulative, demanding, and unappreciative of anything and everything you do for them. You guarantee they will grow up believing they can do as they please, that it's unfair of you to expect them to lift a finger of responsibility around the home, and that it's your duty to give them every-thing they want and serve them in every conceivable way. Putting children first in the family further guarantees that you will experience parenthood as one of the most frustrating and unrewarding things you've ever done. It further guarantees the ultimate unhappiness of your children.[3]

Give your children the luxury of seeing one parent who loves the other unconditionally. This will serve them well when they face the challenges of marriage themselves. Give your mate a place of honor in your home. If you're divorced, refuse to say anything negative about your former mate.

There is no marriage so cold that it cannot be warmed. By God's grace, my (Connie) marriage was transformed. Those dreaded "How come…?" questions don't surface anymore. In fact, just this week my daughter said to me, "Dad is so sweet—he came home from work yes-terday and the first thing he said was 'Where's your mother? I've missed her and want to see her.'"

"I've missed her and want to see her."

Are those beautiful words or what? With God's help, we experi-enced a miracle in our marriage…and we pray that you will too!

❧

Bottom Line: Loving your spouse is one of the greatest treasures you can give your children.

CHAPTER FIVE

WAKE UP ON THE RIGHT SIDE OF THE BED

A Personal Check on Beginning Your Days Right

It's no fun to talk to my mom if she's irritable or moody.

RHEA, 14

❧

Are you hypersensitive? Do you frequently wake up on the wrong side of the bed? Have you noticed members of your family trying to avoid you? If so, your kids may be feeling like they're walking on eggshells around you. And since no one is at ease while trying to balance on a bunch of eggshells, your irritability is probably shutting down communication with your family.

I (Connie) remember one morning when I was especially sharp with our thirteen-year-old daughter—all morning long. I thought she dallied too long at breakfast, loitered too much in front of the mirror, and sauntered far too slowly to the car. She really hadn't done anything wrong; she just moved like she always moves. She simply doesn't "hurry" in the same way I do—in fact, she simply doesn't hurry at all, ever!

In reality, I was the one who had the problem that morning. I was tired and had gotten up on the wrong side of the bed. So all morning, in numerous ways, I told her that she couldn't do anything right.

I continued snipping at her while I drove her to school. But then, just as she was getting out of the car in front of the school, I suddenly felt bad about how I had treated her all morning.

So what did I do when these feelings of guilt washed over me? I pasted a big smile on my face, warmed up my voice, perked up my eyes, and said, "Have a wonderful day!" She looked at me like I'd just sprung a second head! Did my daughter recognize my attempt to clear my conscience for the day? Of course she did!

Thinking of this reminds me of the time when a friend's father-in-law chewed everyone out right before they opened their Christmas presents. He ranted and raved about how unthankful they all were and how much trouble it was to have them over.

"You have no idea how much work all this is for your mother, how much food we have to buy, how much laundry adds up, how much our electric bill skyrockets, and how tired we end up." Then he finished his tirade by adding, "And I hope each of you has a Merry Christmas."

Both of these examples of irritability and insensitivity illustrate how silly it is to think that a barrage of negative statements can be swiped away by one positive afterthought. And we wonder why so many wounded kids are being churned out by families today?

Experts say it takes anywhere from seven to twenty positive statements to counter the effects of one negative one. Imagine the math on just one morning of getting up on the wrong side of the bed!

So if we put these two illustrations together, I could say that after I'd been on Maddi's back all morning long, I "wished her a Merry Christmas." I can't remember what she said, if anything, as she got out of the car to begin her day at school. But I do know that as I watched her disappear through the doors of the school, I was haunted by the thought, *She deserves better than what I gave her today.* And she did.

My stomach had this terrible sinking sensation—commonly known as conviction. Or maybe guilt. Or shame.

In my case, it was all three.

I felt terrible.

I don't know why I didn't run after that child and apologize to her before she ever set foot in that building. But I didn't. Instead, I drove home. And for the next eight hours a black cloud hovered just outside my heart. Looking back, I can surely tell you that *gloomy winter* days may be hard indeed, but *gloomy heart* days are far more difficult.

When Maddi came home that afternoon, I apologized and told her that she hadn't done anything wrong.

When I told her that I had simply gotten up on the wrong side of the bed, her face lit up with a wide grin. She did what kids do so often—and what we adults would do well to learn: She forgave and forgot…and told me all about her day.

I'm sure that if I had stayed camped on the wrong side of the bed after she came home from school, she wouldn't have shared a single thing with me about what had gone on in her day. And who could blame her?

Have you ever heard the saying, "Sometimes I wake up grumpy, and sometimes I let him sleep"? We parents would do well to remember that it's no fun talking to Grumpy. Teenagers communicate best in an environment where they feel safe, secure, and accepted. But when their home life is a minefield of our negativism—even when we think we're hounding them for their own good—our teens may put up with us, but they will also shut up…for their own good.

While reading this, have you been piqued by the realization that you have been out of sorts a lot of the time? If so, it's time to assess what's going on in your life and make some changes. Teens simply don't enjoy talking to people, especially parents, who are always in a bad mood.

⤝⤞

Bottom Line: When you get out of bed, make sure Mr. Grumpy doesn't come with you.

CHAPTER SIX

MORE THAN FOOD AND CLOTHING

Is Your Teen's Heart and Soul Well Dressed?

*I'm really open with my parents.
I know they want the best for me, so I really value their opinion.*

DEBORAH, 16

❧

I (Connie) have long said that my dad was a twenty-first-century parent way before his time. What do I mean? Even though two of my sisters and I were born in the fifties, he had a modern-day approach to parenting. How? He recognized the importance, even then, of letting us know we were hugely important in his life. Most dads "back then" thought their major responsibilities were to feed and clothe their families. My dad, though he took these responsibilities seriously, knew there was something far more important: feeding and clothing our hearts and souls as well.

So nearly every evening when he came home from work, he would play "bat and ball" with me and my sisters in our front yard. He went through the painstaking motions of teaching each of us how to hit and catch the ball, throw someone out at first base, pick off the lead runner, tag up, and all the rest. During these baseball training sessions with Dad, my mom always sat on the front porch and cheered us on. The fact that each of us played high school sports is a credit to him.

His ultimate goal, however, wasn't to raise athletes. Actually, it was to let us know how important we were to him. You see, when we played ball, we did far more than just play ball. We talked and chatted between innings. We laughed and joked about things that had gone on during the day. We might even share how someone had hurt our feelings or made fun of how we had struck out during a game when the girls had taken on the boys at recess. When we did, my dad would say, "That's okay, you'll get 'em next time." I cannot remember a single time when he made fun of us or of our feelings in any way. He and my mother were there to guide us and to reassure us at every turn, consistently letting us know how special we were to them. Because of this, our love and respect for them knew no limits and continue to grow even today—many years later.

Do your kids know how special they are to you? Do they know that you believe in them? When they experience failure, do you assure them that they'll "get 'em next time"? Are you doing more than meeting only their physical needs? Are you clothing their hearts and souls so warmly, wondrously, and completely that they would consider themselves to be candidates for a "Best-Dressed Kids" list?

Heidi, a girl Kathy and I (Kent) worked with for years, wouldn't have come close to making this list. Almost everything her mother said to her was negative. She was critical about her friends, fashion, weight, hairstyle...everything. It wasn't overt criticism, but came more in the form of snide, cynical remarks. Small discourtesies. Little disrespectful comments. Rude responses. She rarely felt like her mother cared about her heart. In fact, she felt as if her heart were being stripped bare, chunk by chunk by chunk. By the time Heidi was sixteen, she simply wouldn't listen to her mom anymore...about anything. Each time she talked with me and Kathy about issues in her life, we would try to persuade her to talk with her mom. Yet every time she'd roll her eyes and say, "Yeah, right," and then launch into a twenty-minute tirade on how much she despised her. Even if her mom had wanted to invest in her life, Heidi no longer trusted her. And in times of crisis, Heidi's withered soul shrank away from her mother.

Deborah's relationship with her parents was totally different from this. She never hesitated telling us how easily she expressed love to her parents: "I'm really open with my parents. I know they want the best for me, so I really value their opinion." What was the difference? Deborah's parents wisely spent time nurturing her soul with love—she knew they deeply cared about what was going on in her life. Day after day they...

- did little acts of kindness for her
- listened without judging
- talked to her like an adult
- treated her with respect and courtesy
- actively supported her pursuits
- ate dinners together as a family
- spent time with her and her sisters

Each action said to her, "You are special to us." What's more, when they occasionally made a mistake in parenting, Deborah was pretty forgiving. "Sure they make mistakes. But when they're wrong, they're quick to apologize. Plus, I know they only want what's best for me, so little screwups are no big deal."

By the way, guess who Deborah talked to about issues in her life? Her parents! When she talked with me and Kathy about something important, it was usually at the urging of her parents. Since she was such an active member of our group and her parents trusted us, they often counseled her to get our advice. We were added voices instead of replacement voices.

So here's the deal: If you want to influence your teen, she has to know that you care just as much about the needs of her heart as you do about her physical needs. How do you do this? By consistently letting her know just how special she is to you on a day-in-and-day-out basis. If she feels like you're tending her soul, the love between you will deepen. And when love grows, conversation flows.

❧

Bottom Line: Take up gardening: Lovingly tend the soil of your teen's heart.

CHAPTER SEVEN

A Promise Is a Promise

Can Your Teen Trust Your Word?

*The thing I respect most about my parents is
that their word is their bond. Always.*

CATHERINE, 19

❧

One of the best things you can do as a parent is to occasionally ask your teen this question: "Have I ever made a promise to you that I didn't keep?"

Asking this may seem like you're sticking your neck out a bit, and you are! But avoiding the subject won't change the facts. Even if you don't discuss it, your teenager is well aware of any promises you haven't delivered on.

Bringing up the topic and inviting your kids' input does four things:

- It allows you to see things through their eyes. Many parents are amazed to discover that what they thought was said in passing was taken very seriously by their children.
- It allows you to address the problem and give your input on what was said. In a sense, it allows teens to see the situation through your eyes.
- It gives you the opportunity to rectify the situation, if needed.
- It's a great reminder to watch your words carefully in the future!

My (Connie) husband and I have done this several times over the years, thinking each time that there was no way we'd made any promises that we hadn't delivered on. But to our surprise, the first time we asked, they said, "Yes! Dad said that one day soon we'd visit Florida, and we never have."

They were right! Even though this had slipped his mind for some time, he recalled making that specific comment. My husband remembered telling them that, but had long since forgotten about it. Not long thereafter, he needed to take a business trip to Orlando, so we decided to make it a family affair—strictly for the purpose of honoring our word to our daughters.

On another occasion, our daughters said that when they were younger we had told them we'd build them a playhouse in the backyard if we ever bought a home (we were renting at the time). A lightbulb began to turn on in our brains—even though the bulb was dimly lit and low wattage, the recollection was there. By this time, the girls were too old to want a playhouse anymore—they were teens—so my husband asked them what he could do to clear his account with them. They jokingly suggested a trip to Europe. He countered with a shopping trip to their favorite store. They agreed. A playhouse will never be part of their memories, but they will know that their dad did his best to honor his word.

At first glance it may seem like your child is the primary beneficiary from these assessments and clearing of accounts, but you can be sure that you will be the one to benefit most. It will help restore any trust in you that was lost and let your teens know that you are committed to being a person who is true to your word. Who isn't drawn to a person who keeps his word? Just about everyone we know of—including teens.

～

Bottom Line: A broken promise is much like a broken bone. It hurts, but can heal nicely with the right treatment.

Chapter Eight

Simplify Your Life

Are You Too Busy or Too Stressed to Talk?

*If you knew your life would end tomorrow, what
would you change today? Go ahead and change it whether
you die tomorrow or not. You'll never regret that you did.*

Ora, 90

Benjamin Franklin once said that two things in life were certain—
death and taxes. Recently, everyone from pastors to disc jockeys has
added a third certainty: stress.

Just a few days ago I (Connie) pulled into the middle school park-
ing lot to pick my daughter up from play practice. Since the session
was running late and I'd been running around all day long, I reclined
my seat, lay back, and closed my eyes. After five minutes or so, I put
the seat back up into its regular position so my daughter could easily
see me. As I watched for her, I couldn't help but notice the other parents in cars near mine. Amazingly, the majority of them had reclined
their seats and were resting with their eyes closed.

We are a tired society, I thought to myself. *Tired and growing more
tired.*

Stress and busyness have a way of wearing us out—making us feel
even more tired than we are—and we're probably tired enough as it is.
Stressed-out people aren't much fun to talk to either. If you don't
believe it, ask your teens if this is true for them. They will probably say
that stressed-out people (or parents) often seem too preoccupied, too
hurried, and too easily distracted to listen.

Are you giving your kids the impression that you don't care a
whole lot about what they're saying to you? Do you often pretend to
listen to them, but the glaze in your eyes says otherwise? Your younger

children may not notice, but most teens pick up on this distance very quickly.

Frequently, stress is the result of schedule overload. A single item by itself is usually not overwhelming. But collectively, individual items have a way of adding up to overload. We soon begin to feel overwhelmed. And even when doubt about whether we can do it all begins to overshadow us, we try to do it all anyway. Driven, goal-oriented, type-A personalities are especially vulnerable to this tendency. We may indeed end up getting everything done that we thought we needed to do, but all too often our completion of tasks comes at the expense of heavily draining the quality of our relationships.

To de-stress your life, you may want to try to:

- Keep your "to do" list as short as possible. Put aside nonessential household chores. Few people notice if your baseboards are spotless, your files are perfectly alphabetized, or your closet is organized by size, season, and color.
- Learn to say no. Every need is not a calling. If you're wondering whether you have time to squeeze in one more thing, you don't.
- Keep things in proper perspective. Taking treats to the high school band doesn't have to add up to baking in the kitchen for six hours—baking boxed brownies, using ready-made cookie dough, or buying cookies at the bakery will suffice.
- Hire out whatever your budget allows. For example, twelve-year-old kids are great for planting flowers, baby-sitting, mowing lawns, raking leaves, and even cleaning parts of your house.
- Teach *your* children to take responsibility for some of the chores. Sharing responsibilities is part of the privilege of belonging to a family...and is timeless training for taking on added responsibilities as they grow older.
- Exercise—you'll feel better mentally and physically.
- Get enough rest.
- Eat balanced meals.
- Cancel your magazine subscriptions.
- Do two things at once. Recently I (Connie) determined right

off the bat that a certain phone call was going to end up being a long conversation. Knowing this, I switched to the cordless phone, went outside, and as I talked I pulled the wilted annuals up from the flower beds—a task I'd been dreading for days. However, this chore didn't seem nearly as time-consuming and cumbersome when I coupled it with another activity.

- Pet your dog. Research shows that petting a dog actually decreases stress! However, if you don't already own a dog, it could be that the stress in training one would far outweigh the benefits of petting one. This is strictly our opinion, not actual research!
- Make simple meals for dinner.
- Change your sheets less often.
- Do less laundry. Teach your kids to change out of their "good" outfits and into everyday clothes. If treated properly, clothing does not need to be laundered each and every time it is worn—especially jeans, sweatshirts, dresses, and slacks.
- If you agree to take on an additional responsibility, alleviate yourself of one you already have.
- Stop worrying about things that are beyond your control.
- Stop and smell the roses. Take a few minutes each day to thank the Lord for your life and the blessings you have.

~~~

Bottom Line: Stressed-out parents and talkative teens rarely communicate on the same wavelength.

CHAPTER NINE

LISTENING RIGHT
How to Make Your Teen Feel Heard

There's a difference between listening and really hearing. Few parents really hear what their kids are trying to say.
CASSIDY, 18

⊷

Have you ever noticed how everyone seems to be talking and no one seems to be listening? Never has this been truer than in our busy world today. Some people seem to have a gift of listening, but they are rare. However, the good news is that you can actually learn to become a great listener!

One of the keys to having your teens talk to you is to give them someone worth talking to! Too many teens talk little enough as it is. Give them a detached or preoccupied parent, and they'll talk even less.

Few parents seem to realize the importance of really listening to their teens. How do we know this? We recently surveyed a group of teens and were astonished at the large number of teens who said they wished their parents listened better.

Time and again we heard various takes on the following:

- "I'd be more willing to talk if I felt they really cared about what I had to say."
- "My parents are always nagging me to talk to them, but when I do, they seem annoyed that their sacred routine of reading the paper or watching the news has been interrupted."
- "My parents are too busy to listen."
- "My parents always tell me how I can come to them with anything, but when I try to, all they want to do is get me to hurry up with whatever I'm saying so they can go on with whatever they were doing before I showed up."

41

- "I'm never going to say, 'That's nice, honey,' to my kids. What it really says is, 'I'm too busy to listen to you right now, but I'll pretend I am by this shallow remark.'"
- "My parents say they love me, but I don't feel very loved when they're too busy to listen to me."

Pretty sobering thoughts on the hearts of these teens, aren't they? If you haven't been a good listener in the past, it's time to start today. And if you've been pretty good at listening, why not commit to becoming even better at it?

Here are some listening strategies to try:

1. Look at your teen when he talks to you. If your eyes are focused somewhere else, it will look like your mind is elsewhere too.
2. Eliminate distractions. Turn off the TV, put down the newspaper, et cetera.
3. Lean forward as you listen. Listen with eagerness!
4. Give feedback. Nod, smile, and ask questions.
5. Don't interrupt or change the subject. Give him your undivided attention even if he's talking about something you have no interest in.
6. Allow him to finish his own sentences, and even more important, *don't give solutions unless he asks for them.* Remember, listening doesn't equate to giving advice.
7. Repeat back to him some of the things he said. This is validating and confirming.
8. Compliment him on his wisdom and insight. One of the byproducts of listening is that it provides great material for building up your teen.
9. Show your appreciation. Let him know you appreciate his sharing.

Sometimes you may get confused by what your teen is trying to say, or maybe he's saying one thing, but his body language is saying another. Try enlisting some of these clarifying phrases when this occurs:

- "I'm not sure what you mean—tell me more."
- "Can you give me an example of that?"
- "Why do you feel this is best?"
- "I hear you saying _____. Am I close to what you're telling me or completely out of the ballpark?"
- "What do you mean when you say _____? Define that for me."

Continue to ask short, brief questions until you understand what is being said.

In their book *Parents' Guide to the Spiritual Mentoring of Teens,* Joe White and Jim Weidmann list eight things your teen wants from communication. These include:

- to get your full attention
- to be listened to, from beginning to end, without interruption
- for you to care about what he says
- for her secrets to be kept
- to express his feelings
- to be asked her opinion
- to hear about your own failures
- to hear an understanding of his world

They follow this list up with eight things your teen doesn't want:

- to be talked down to
- to be pushed away
- for you to get in her face
- to be blasted with Bible verses or a sermon
- to be judged or ridiculed for what he says
- to hear unsolicited advice
- for you to freak out
- To hear adult clichés. ("Back when I was your age…," "As long as you're under my roof…," "You don't know how easy you have it….")[4]

Like anything else, if you tell your teen he can always come to you about anything, you're going to have to back it up with your actions.

When he comes to you, put the world on hold, look him lovingly in the eyes, zip your mouth, and turn your ears on high. You won't regret it. If you follow these strategies consistently, your teen will begin to think you really mean it when you say, "You can talk to me about anything."

❧

Bottom Line: Listening requires far more than just your ears—it requires your eyes and heart too!

CHAPTER TEN

LISTENING WRONG

How to Make Your Teen Feel Unheard

*My parents talk about how you're supposed to be slow to speak and
quick to listen, but then they do just the opposite.*

ANNA, 14

⤬

Have you ever been talking to someone and suddenly realized that the
person wasn't "all there" (Their few "uh-huh's" and "oh's" only serving
to confirm your suspicion that while their bodies were present, their
minds were on other things.) How did it feel to be saying something
that was not being heard? Did it make you feel unsettled? Unimportant
to the person? Frustrated? Resolved not to bother talking to the person
again?

How do you think your teen feels when she realizes that you
haven't heard a word she has been saying for the last five minutes?
Unsettled? Unimportant to you? Frustrated? Resolved not to bother
talking to you?

If you want your teen to talk to you, and more important, if you
want her to know that she has your 100 percent attention, we suggest
you avoid being:

1. *The half-ear listener:* This person only hears a small portion of
   what's being said. I (Kent) do this all too frequently. Just recently
   I was multitasking and talking to my wife on the phone. Right
   after she said she missed me and was feeling sad, I said, "Can I
   call you back in five minutes?" She said, "Did you hear what I
   just said?" Obviously I hadn't. If your teen (or anyone else for
   that matter) feels like this very often, she'll stop talking.

2. *The "even though I'm talking to the younger children, I'm still listening" listener.* If you need to tend to your younger child, ask

your teen to "hold that thought" for just a second, tend to the other child, and then quickly turn your attention back to your teen. Your younger children should know that unless they're bleeding, on fire, or uncertain where their next breath is coming from, they are not to interrupt you when you're engaged in a conversation. It is common today to see a four-year-old demand his mother's ear when she's talking to someone else. And it's even more surprising to see the mother put the person on hold while she gives her toddler her undivided attention. This isn't right and does no one any favors—especially the toddler.

3. *The "even though I'm on the phone, I'm still listening" listener.* Enough said.

4. *The "I can carry on two conversations at once" listener.* Maybe you can but you shouldn't.

5. *The "don't let my reading the newspaper keep you from talking" listener.* More than enough said!

6. *The "walk in and out of the room while you're talking" listener.* "Wanderers" aren't good listeners—wandering tells your teen that other things take priority over listening to her.

7. *The "I'm going to just rest my eyes a bit" listener.* About the time our kids hit the teen years, our bodies hit the need for more rest! If you want your teen to talk, you need to stay awake!

8. *The "I can do at least six other things while you're talking" listener.* Doing this is like handing her a written invitation that says, "Find someone else to talk to; I'm busy." More than likely, she will.

9. *The "interrupts constantly" listener.* Place your hand over your mouth if you must, but let your teen finish her sentences and thoughts.

10. *The "I'll listen for thirty seconds" listener."* Don't give your teen your undivided attention for just a moment or two, but then turn away. This is the proverbial "carrot dangle." It teaches your teen not to open up in the first place—why bother?

11. *The "I can and will correct everything you say before you finish saying it, especially if it involves criticism of me" listener.* Let's face it—it's not particularly fun to be criticized in general, but it's even less fun when the criticism comes from our teens.

Parents, hear this: Listen carefully to what your teen says all of the time, but listen extra carefully when you find it especially tough to listen, and then measure your words carefully.

Because it negates your teen's expression of her thoughts, defending yourself at every turn is the quickest way to freeze a conversation. On some occasions she will be so off base that you'll want to discuss the issues (notice we didn't say, "You'll want to blow her ideas to bits"). As you keep in mind the importance of remaining open and approachable, also remember that at times she will be closer to the target than you are.

A quick example: She may feel your curfew rules are too stringent. You come back with, "You stay out much later than I ever did, and besides that, nothing good ever happens after midnight anyway."

Her reason for requesting the later curfew hours may actually be based on the fact that she wants to take a couple of friends with her to the Fifth Quarter youth meetings that are held at your church after the high school football game. However, if she takes her friends home after the meetings, she'd break curfew by thirty minutes. Is this worth considering? It would seem so.

Teens enjoy talking to the right kind of listener. Be one of them. By being a good listener you will

- provide a safe atmosphere for your teen to share,
- give her the confidence to say what's on her mind, and most of all,
- show her that you highly value what she is saying. This validation will stay with her for a lifetime.

⤳

Bottom Line: If a good listener is truly a work of art, would your teen consider you a masterpiece?

WHY IS OUR ANGEL ACTING LIKE A PRIMATE?

*A Sneak Peek at Today's Teenager
and the Youth Culture*

⤳

No, you're not crazy. Something is definitely happening to your little angel. He's growing up and will soon emerge as an adult. But first, the teenage years! Yet being a teenager isn't exactly the same as it was back in the dinosaur days when we were teens. Sure, we also had the developmental challenges that teens face today. But when we consider all that's bearing down on our children—technology, the media, drugs, the Internet, and changing societal values—we begin to see that our kids are facing stress factors that we never could have dreamed of when we were their age.

Let's continue our parental reality check by taking a sneak peek at the world in which our kids live today. For most parents, this part of the reality check will actually be a wake-up call because we're going to be looking at both the good and the bad.

But don't skip this part and go straight to the more practical stuff that you may be more comfortable and familiar with. Why? Because this quick glimpse of the tricky terrain kids must navigate every day will help you guide them on their journey.

So, are you ready to take off the geriatric blindfold that most parents wear? Then let's begin….

CHAPTER ELEVEN

DEVELOPMENTALLY SPEAKING

Helping Your Teen Navigate the Chaos

*Go easy on me. You have no idea how much drama
I have to deal with every day. I don't think
I could take one more thing!*

AIMEE, 14

Simply put, the teenage years are a journey of transition between child-hood and adulthood. And because the preteen and early teenage years are especially tumultuous, many parents tend to hide their heads in the sand, hoping it will all be over soon. But staying in denial about just how rough the terrain is for our kids is not the answer. Sure, it is an option—but it is not the right one. For starters, understanding the drastic changes that occur in the young people themselves—within a short one- to two-year time frame—will help us better appreciate what they are experiencing and why they do some of the crazy things they do.

THE CHAOS

Physical

As one teenage girl said, "When will it end—so I can just have a body that looks the same from one week to the next?"[5] Invariably, before boys begin to experience the slightest physical changes, most girls are well on their way to becoming women. The transformation from little girl to young lady can be rather traumatic, often making girls feel awk-ward and out of place. Guys eventually begin to sprout as well, and when this happens, look out! During their transitional phase, life con-sists of little more than eating, sleeping, and growing.

While both guys and girls look forward to becoming young men and women, some of the physical changes are downright scary. So as parents, let's not forget just how frightening and intimidating these changes can be. As a youth pastor, I (Kent) occasionally was asked by single mothers in our church to talk to their sons when they hit puberty. I remember a conversation with two brothers in particular. As we talked, they were relieved to realize the "strange" things happening to their bodies were normal. Having someone identify with what was happening to them—one who was willing to share how awkward and anxious he felt when he experienced these same changes—lifted a mammoth weight off their shoulders. They walked away from our time together feeling normal again.

Mental

Perhaps the greatest change that occurs during puberty is cerebral. But unlike the outward physical changes that can't be missed, this mental development frequently goes unnoticed by hurried parents. During early adolescence, teens develop what is called *formal operational thinking*. As this happens, they move from concrete to abstract thought.

When a teen begins thinking abstractly, there is

- a shift from idealism to critical thinking (teens question *everything*)
- a new knack for arguing logically (my parents always said I was a great kid until I became a teenager and developed an opinion)
- an increased aptitude for decision making (although teens remain absolutely indecisive about what to wear)
- an ability to make moral evaluations (yet what they believe is not always backed up by how they live)

While this change is a developmental milestone for teens, it also brings new challenges to parenting.

Emotional

The gargantuan fluctuation in their teens' emotions unnerves even the most savvy parents. But the intense roller-coaster ride and self-centered emotional outbursts are a little more bearable when we are armed with an understanding of what our teens are going through.

Relational

Teenagers are wired for relationships. As children they had *playmates*, but now they want *friends*. This means their peer group now soars to "major player" status. In almost every situation, teenagers unconsciously ask themselves, "Do people, other than those in my own family, like me?" The power of the "audience," whether real or imagined, guides much of their social behavior. Our technologically savvy world widens the challenge because peer groups are no longer geographically limited. While we adults see the Internet as an information gathering tool, teens use it to build a network of friends that often spans the globe.

Spiritual

If faith is important to your family, be prepared for the teenage walk to include doubt, joy, failure, and success. In other words, the faith of teenagers is turbulent—idealistic one moment, dashed the next. In this aspect of their journey to adulthood, they no longer blindly and unquestioningly accept their parents' morals and beliefs. This transition from *blind faith* into *personal faith* makes authentically living out what they believe a daily struggle. Chris, a teenager from New York, recently summed up this common teen struggle when he said, "I really believe in God, so why can't I live for God?"

HELPING TEENS NAVIGATE THE CHAOS

So what's a parent to do? How can we get them to talk to us about what's going on in their hearts, minds, bodies, and spirits—so we can help them navigate the chaos?

Physical

First off, never, ever, ever make fun of physical appearance. Teasing accomplishes nothing. Teach your children to love their bodies just as they are…that week. Second, when talking to your teen about physical changes, steer clear from using slang. Instead, use proper terminology for body parts and speak plainly about the physical development taking place in his life. These words may feel and sound awkward since they're not used in everyday language, but use them anyway. It's a way to show respect for God's physical design.

Mental

Authentically seek your teens' input by encouraging healthy discussions, even debates. Don't give your opinion too quickly. Even more, don't immediately answer questions your teenagers raise. Instead, let them wrestle with issues. Help them develop analytical skills by teaching them to think logically. Finally, help them learn to argue passionately about what they believe (this week) without becoming emotionally charged— by the way, this means we must do this too.

Emotional

Remember that although we don't like seeing our teens on an emotional roller-coaster ride, at least we aren't on it ourselves. But they are…and it's often a 24/7 struggle for them! Therefore, show compassion. If they know we're trying to understand and help them, they'll *want* to talk to us and will be more apt to listen to our suggestions on how they can keep a better handle on their emotions.

Relational

Give them space to search for their personal identity—within reason, of course. In other words, be involved in their lives without smothering them. Also, remember that teenagers—especially early adolescents—*try on* different personalities. Don't fight these experiments. Instead, help them assess which personality expressions are admirable and which are "whacked-out."

Spiritual

Since more is caught than taught, authentically model your own faith.

〰

Bottom Line: Remember, young teens are developmental rookies. When they make mistakes, cut them some slack and encourage them to talk with you about their feelings.

CHAPTER TWELVE

I WANT TO BE ME

The Importance of Individuality and Autonomy

*My parents are like mosquitoes, little by little
they suck the life out of me.* [6]
NATE, 13

❧

As they seek to become their own persons, teenagers are in a relational tug-of-war with their parents. During this time of struggle, kids usually say that they aren't severing the ties with their parents, but instead are only seeking their own identity. Wise parents accept this and understand the importance of releasing their kids *gradually*.

This common parent/teen tension is rooted in the fact that most teens can't comprehend why their parents won't give them complete independence *right now*, but their parents know the wisdom of not giving their kids more freedom than they can handle. The result? A relational tug-of-war until the teens finally reach adulthood and leave the proverbial parental nest!

TAKE A PERSONAL INVENTORY

So how do parents help young people traverse this tricky journey? How do we grant them independence gradually? We start by taking personal inventory of our current parenting paradigm. For instance, when do you think teenagers should have the right to make choices about

- the clothes they wear,
- the music they listen to,
- the movies they watch,
- the "style" of their bedrooms (this not only includes decor, but whether it looks immaculate or like a war zone),

- how they spend their money,
- how they wear their hair,
- their curfew,
- who they can hang out with,
- what church, if any, they attend, and
- tattoos or piercings.

Clearly, there is no single answer to these issues. What's more, there's a good chance that our approach will differ from teen to teen. But don't kid yourself: These *will* be issues and turning a blind eye only ripens the environment for rebellion. Whether we admit it or not, our teens are on the path to autonomy, and we need to aid them in their journey. Taking inventory of our current inclinations is the place to start.

DECLARATION OF INDEPENDENCE

The next step is to help our teens develop a plan for independence. Once they reach the teen years, we can no longer be passive. We must proactively decide how—and at what pace—we will let go. In summation, we must ask ourselves what steps will we take and when. Clearly, there are no easy answers. However, here are a few ways for helping your teens draft their declaration of independence:

- *Allow baby steps.* Let your early adolescent assert herself in little ways early on. For instance, let her decorate her room, pick out her clothes, and choose her hairstyle. These actions tell her: "We want you to discover who you are."
- *Map out an age-appropriate plan.* Don't wait until topics like dating and curfew become major issues; decide your guidelines early and articulate them often. In fact, the earlier and more often, the better! One set of parents we know started telling their nine-year-old that she wasn't allowed to date until she was sixteen. When dating became an issue when she turned fourteen, her parents had five years of history on their side.
- *Be incremental.* Teenagers are rookies at decision-making. Consequently, giving too much freedom too early guarantees teens will make decisions they will regret for years to come.

Since early adolescents aren't capable of making major decisions on their own, expecting them to do so is unfair.

On the flip side, too little freedom too late is just as catastrophic and leads to rebellion. The parents of one guy we know granted him virtually no freedom while he was in high school. But then when he graduated, they said, "You're on your own." He went bananas and nearly ruined his life.

Both approaches—too much freedom too early and too little freedom too late—are recipes for disaster.

- *Connect freedom with responsibility.* My (Kent) parents were great at this! The more responsible my behavior, the more freedom I was granted. For instance, when my curfew was raised from eleven to midnight, there was no problem if I came home at midnight. However, if I strolled in around 12:20, I lost my privilege of the later curfew. What made this approach especially effective was that my parents actually enforced the consequence (what a foreign concept).

- *Don't give privileges away.* In my home, playing sports was considered a privilege. My parents made it clear that making certain grades and attending church were prerequisites to participating in sports activities. If I dropped the ball in either of those two areas, I was off the basketball or soccer team. Driving was also a privilege. In order to drive, I was required to obey traffic laws and pay for my own auto insurance and gas.

  I also want to point out that because my parents limited their expectations to a few essentials, I never felt overwhelmed. At the same time, they expected me to consistently follow through on my responsibilities and commitments. This approach taught me that opportunity is attached to responsibility.

- *Allow consequences.* Don't overprotect teens. Instead, allow them to experience natural consequences. If they break something, they should pay for it. If they commit to a specific activity and then a better opportunity comes along, make sure they fulfill their original commitment. Help them learn firsthand the role of discretion in decision making.

- *Ask for input.* Finally, you might be surprised to learn that teens are often tougher on themselves than their parents are. While they crave freedom, they also want protection and provision—clear indications that they are genuinely loved. So while teens don't ask for boundaries directly, they long for them.

  When you allow teens to give their input on boundaries and guidelines (and ask for their views on rewards and consequences), you will find them opening up and talking to you more freely…and they will give you some great ideas!

Bottom Line: Help your teen write her "declaration of independence."

CHAPTER THIRTEEN

TECHNOLOGICALLY ADVANCED, MEDIA NUMBED

Facing the Giants of Youth Culture

The door has been left wide open and unlocked by many parents.
WALT MUELLER IN *UNDERSTANDING TODAY'S YOUTH CULTURE*
(PARAPHRASE)

❧

Technologically advanced, media numbed. Bill Clem, a friend with twenty-five years of experience working with high school students, first used this phrase in a presentation on contemporary student issues. When I heard it, I (Kent) almost stood up in the middle of the seminar and shouted, "That's it! That's *the* word picture I've been looking for."

Technology and media (music, movies, television, and magazines) are *the* two Goliaths of youth culture. These days, teens can't imagine life without computers, cell phones, digital technology, or CDs. These two giants saturate their world.

Is this necessarily bad? Some believe so. Many point fingers at media and technology, blaming them for practically every cultural woe. Yet an honest appraisal brings the realization that neither is all evil. Likewise, neither is all good. In reality, both are neutral. Actually, the degree of evil or good lies in the content of what is channeled through these technological giants.

As parents it's easy to use these giants as scapegoats for all the turmoil teens face. Yet as Walt Mueller says, if "the door was left unlocked and wide open" by parents, we are just as responsible.[7] So here's the deal: a significant role for today's parents is to train teens to think critically about how these tools are used. Such training will produce technologically advanced, media-savvy teens who refuse to be mind-numbed robots.

Wondering how to design this training? Here are a few ideas to get your gears cranking:

- *Evaluate your life.* People today rarely contemplate the values they embrace. Instead, we fill our out-of-control, hyperdrive lives with lots of activity, leaving very little time for reflection.

  However, to develop savvy teens, we must first know who we are and what we believe. What's more, we must actually live what we think we believe.

- *Don't run for your life.* When overwhelmed with the dangers of technology and media, some parents "bunker down" and don't allow any television or computers into their home (or should we say fortress). This separation tactic actually ends up backfiring when teens occasionally slip out of the bunker or when they grow up and escape for good.

  Since we can't control their environment for the rest of their lives, facing the danger head-on is a better approach. So, let technology and media into your house, but be alert and cautious. One set of parents we know tackles it like this: "Our kids are not allowed to have TVs or computers with Internet access in their rooms. These are set up in our den so use can be supervised."

- *Don't sleep your life away.* Here, parents ignore danger by doing nothing. And although teens might pretend they like limitless freedom, most feel unloved when parents don't care enough to protect them.

  A better tactic is to set boundaries that allow you to influence the discernment of your teen. Expand these boundaries as their discernment grows and their values deepen.

- *Watch your life.* What do you watch on TV or look at over the Internet? How many hours do you spend in front of each machine? What kind of music do you enjoy? Are the lyrics acceptable? When modeling values to your children, keep in mind that teens usually do in excess what they see and hear their parents doing in moderation (now that's a scary thought).

- *Get connected to their lives.* Above all, be proactive.

First, know what's happening in the major media that shapes their world. For example, browse through *Rolling Stone* and *Entertainment Weekly* magazines. Catch a glimpse of VH1 from time to time. Log on to screenit.com for movie reviews. Even sit down with your teens and watch what they have been watching. A friend of ours, Jim, does this pretty regularly with his teenagers. He doesn't turn off the television or walk away in disgust when something he doesn't like appears on the screen. Instead, he talks with his kids and helps them think critically about what they are watching. While his kids might chide him for being old-fashioned, they have told us in private that they know their dad is doing a good thing. So be like Jim. Ask your teens to point out the false presentations of reality and empty promises on the screen. If you listen to them with sincerity and respect their opinions, you might be surprised at how teachable they are.

Also, be aware of Internet dangers. Again, by pure definition the Internet is neither good nor bad. But parents must keep in mind that using it recklessly can wreak havoc.

I (Kent) recently spoke with two guys who are addicted to pornography and use the Internet to get their daily fixes. I also know a girl who developed a virtual romantic relationship and tried to run away from home. We hope these stories scare you, because these kids were normal, everyday teenagers.

In short, be proactive about helping your teens make healthy choices when they use the Internet! For example, limit and monitor its use. Use parental control functions that limit access to objectionable sites and e-mail filters that limit temptations from popping up on your child's screen. And by all means, keep Internet access in a high-traffic room that allows the users to have adequate privacy but also makes harmful activities more challenging to hide.

❧

Bottom Line: Be proactive: Get connected and stay connected.

CHAPTER FOURTEEN

PREVENT DEFENSE

Teenagers and Substance Abuse

*Adults don't understand how widespread drug use is and
how accessible drugs and alcohol are.
Sure, they had drugs back in their day, but
the world has totally changed.*

JIM, 17

⮑

Do you ever feel like you're treading water in a rushing river of information? Yes, there are studies and statistics on every topic these days.

This is especially true of substance abuse. You may be thinking, *I need to talk to my teen about drugs and alcohol, but where do I begin?* You start searching, but all too soon you're overwhelmed by a flood of information. It makes you want to throw up your hands and shout, "I quit!"

But here's a thought. Don't worry too much about what the latest experts are saying. Basically, most are saying the same thing: *Drugs are dangerous, and addictions ruin lives.* But to find out more, visit the Web for about an hour and gather some basic information. This approach will give you all you need to start talking to your teen about the dangers of drugs.

But once you have information, you're still left with this question: How do I talk about this stuff? Here are a few thoughts that will help you navigate these conversations:

"BE"

First, make sure you're "being" the person you need to be to influence your teen. Are you *being*

- *a builder?* Do you have a meaningful relationship with your teen? How much time are you spending together?

- *an example?* Again, the phrase "more is caught than taught" comes to mind here. What's your teen "catching" from you?
- *a teacher?* Don't leave drug education to schools or television. Take responsibility and *be* a teacher.
- *a listener?* Do you lecture, or do you communicate through an exchange of talking *and* listening?
- *an initiator?* Be proactive about initiating these kinds of conversations.

MAKE IT PERSONAL

The next step to talking with your teen about drugs and alcohol is to make it personal. Do you know kids are attracted to substances for different reasons?

- Peer Pressure…"All my friends do it, so I *had* to try it if I wanted to fit in."
- Curiosity…"I've always wondered how marijuana would make me feel."
- Risk-taking…"The rush of buying is half the thrill."
- Fun-seeking…"Hey, I'm bored and drinking is fun."
- Self-confidence…"Drinking helps me loosen up at parties."
- Rebellion…"I do drugs to get back at my parents."
- Escapism…"Getting high helps me forget how much life stinks."

Do you know what environmental factors or personality traits might contribute to the likelihood for your teen to experiment with drugs? One father told us, "All four of our kids are different. Our oldest is cautious, the next is adventurous, the third is a politician, and our baby is definitely a clown." Each of the kids he describes here would be tempted for different reasons. Keep this in mind when talking with your teen. Tailor the conversations to the particular personality.

RECOGNIZE PHASES

"When my son went through bumpy times with friends, I knew he was more susceptible to escapism than usual. And when he was invited to all those parties during his junior year, he told me the temptation to drink went way up."

At certain times in their lives, kids are more susceptible to drugs or alcohol. So, be particularly alert if your teen is facing difficulties like getting cut from a sports team or breaking up with a girlfriend. However, it's important to also be attentive during good times. For example, if he suddenly becomes part of the "in" crowd, he might be lured to experiment just to fit in. Usually, any significant change can make teens more vulnerable to drinking alcohol or taking drugs.

BASIC DOS AND DON'TS

Finally, here are some dos and don'ts to follow when talking with teens about drugs and alcohol.

- Do ask where your teens are going and what they'll be doing. It *is* your business.
- Do set a curfew and enforce it.
- Don't overreact. Sometimes kids say pretty outrageous things. If we overreact, discussion is instantly cut off. Respond calmly.
- Do get to know your teen's friends. They have a pretty big influence in your child's life.
- Don't crowd teens out of your life. Spend time together. Eat meals together. It's a common belief that families who spend significant amounts of time together have kids who are less likely to be involved in risky behavior.
- Do be careful of "high-risk hours." Drug use is at a high point between the hours when school lets out and parents get home. Figure out ways to supervise your teens during these times.
- Don't hand teens a book and tell them to come to you with questions. Talk face-to-face.
- Do talk about dangers. Explain how drugs hurt people:
    physically…people who do drugs look worn out and are at risk for all kinds of diseases.
    emotionally…drug users are reclusive, moody, and opportunistic.
    educationally…drugs burn brain cells, make it harder to

concentrate, and keep people from graduating (many dropouts are druggies).

professionally…drug addicts have pretty limited career options.

economically…it cost a lot to do drugs.

- Don't lecture. Have ongoing conversations.
- Do use teachable moments. Ask questions when the subject comes up, like during television shows or commercials.
- Don't make rules you won't enforce.
- Do set up rules in advance, and follow through with consequences.
- Most of all, do be clear that drug and alcohol use are not acceptable. Many parents never come right out and say this.

❧

Bottom Line: Take the initiative on this one…talk to your teens early and often about drugs and alcohol.

CHAPTER FIFTEEN

DECODING
POSTMODERNISM

Looking through the Postmodern Lens

It depends on what the meaning of the word is is.
PRESIDENT BILL CLINTON, FIFTY-SOMETHING

Postmodernism.

Have you heard this term tossed around? Do you know what it means?

Postmodernism is not a code name for a specific generation (like Gen X or Millennial Kids). It's also not a passing fad that's here today, gone tomorrow. In a word, postmodernism is a worldview.

Wondering what a worldview is? James Sire describes it as: *a set of basic presuppositions* (assumptions which may be true, partially true, or entirely false), *which we hold* (consciously or subconsciously, consistently or inconsistently) *about the makeup of our world.*[8]

To get a better handle on worldviews, think of them as eyeglasses. In this analogy, each of us chooses a pair of specs to wear. This set of spectacles serves as a filter that significantly influences how we view reality. Different prescriptions (types of glass) cause people to see different realities.

So why is postmodernism suddenly such a big deal? Because this view is so radically different from the worldview specs that most parents wear. The dissimilarities between parents and teens today are philosophical—not just generational—and it is crucial for parents to grasp the rudiments of the postmodern view. If we don't, we won't understand (or communicate effectively) with our teens.

This chapter doesn't focus on getting teens to talk. Rather, it's a peek into their worldview. From the outset, it is important to recognize that they see the world very differently than we do. Yet hopefully the snapshots below will help you catch a glimpse of how teenagers see reality.

REFLECTIONS ON POSTMODERN "TRUTHS"

Truth

The way one deals with truth is perhaps the most significant difference between postmodernism and the worldview lenses most parents wear. As Marv Penner writes: "To the modern mind, a declaration of propositional truth is the starting point for understanding relationships, feelings, and expressions. Kids today see it in a whole different way. They'll tell you that it's in their relationships, experiences, and emotions that they can encounter and discover truth."9 So truth is relative and experiential. No belief system is truer than another. Relativism is not a new phenomenon; however, it's entrenched in the postmodern culture.

Finding Truth

In postmodernism, spirituality is "in." However, since all belief systems are equally valid, all lead to truth. So any attempt to find the one, true belief system is a waste of time. Instead, people are encouraged to find what's truth *for them*.

Communicating Truth

If you were to join a book discussion at your local coffee shop you would probably hear the group facilitator ask, "What does the book say to you?" This illustrates how communication is viewed by those who see through postmodern lenses. In essence, there is no final meaning in communication because words are void of meaning. Millard Erickson describes it this way: "Meaning is thought by some to reside, not objectively in the words and expressions themselves, but in the person who receives them."10

Remember Bill Clinton's response during the Monica Lewinski depositions? "It depends on what the meaning of the word *is* is." That response fits perfectly in a postmodern culture! Readers and hearers, rather than the words, are the final arbiters.

Living Truth

Pragmatism, not morality, is king in postmodernism. Decisions are based on the need of the moment. Whatever works is championed.

Tolerating Truth

The chief ethic of postmodernism is a new tolerance. Tolerance once meant respecting the beliefs of others, even if you did not accept the beliefs. The new definition means all beliefs, lifestyles, and truth-claims must be viewed as equally valid. In fact, the only intolerable sin is saying someone's belief is wrong.

HELPING TEENS BY RESPONDING TO POSTMODERN "TRUTH"

So how do we, as parents, help teens respond to the postmodern paradigm shift taking place in Western culture?

First, let's not stick our heads in the sand or try to bring back the "good old days." Postmodernism is here to stay, so let's deal with it.

Second, we should examine our kids' lives (as well as our own) to see if the radical tendencies of postmodernism have clouded their thinking (and ours). We must help them examine their worldview assumptions (many won't even know they've made assumptions). And we need to encourage them to push their supposition to logical conclusions to see if it's *legit* or not.

For instance, seventeen-year-old Diane once said to me, "Kent, Sarah is so sincere in her beliefs. Her religion must be as real as ours, or else she wouldn't be so committed." Diane couldn't see the intellectual shallowness of her statement. Sincerity is important, but not nearly as important as truth. People can sincerely believe something, yet be sincerely mistaken. Helping teens be intellectually honest is so critical, yet very difficult, in a pluralistic culture such as ours. Perhaps the best way to encourage intellectual honesty is to ask questions:

- Can opposing truth-claims be equally valid?
- How could all paths lead to God?
- Can we tolerate someone's belief and still think he or she is wrong?

Such questions should challenge teenagers to think deeply about their worldview as well as give us a chance to shape it.

Finally, parents should wholeheartedly embrace postmodernism's stronger virtues. For instance, the belief that truth often lies beyond human reason should be applauded. Also, acknowledging that science will never be able to answer every question is a great step forward. Other positives associated with postmodernism include its emphasis on community, spirituality, authenticity, and personal experience.

In spite of its grave philosophical errors, the postmodern worldview also contains some great attributes. So rather than putting your head in the sand and missing out on the opportunity to genuinely help your teen shape his basic values and worldview, help him embrace the good and let go of the bad.

❧

Bottom Line: Help your teen hone his worldview. Be the needle that points north on his worldview compass.

LINGUISTIC LESSONS

Learning to Talk with (Not at) Your Teen

≈

If there is one major mistake parents make, it's *how* they talk to their teens. When our children first arrived, we had a parent/young child relationship with them. But now that they've become teens, the relationship needs to transition into one of parent/young adult, and this can be a tricky thing! All sorts of unexpected twists are in the road and plenty of hairpin turns too! But if we grow discouraged or blasé and don't make the needed adjustments, we'll end up talking *at* our teen instead of *with* our teen. Or maybe not talking at all. And this, dear friend, is a disastrous mistake.

The following chapters are jam-packed with linguistic lessons. You'll find lots of practical skills that will help you talk *with* your teen—an all too rare occurrence in many households today. Become a rarity! In doing so, you'll most likely discover a relationship with your teen that's just waiting to be tapped into.

CHAPTER SIXTEEN

CHOOSE YOUR
BATTLES WISELY

Or You'll Be Fighting All the Time

Home should be a place where you can just be yourself.
CAMERON, 18

⤫

Learning to choose your battles wisely will help ensure that small, petty differences don't regularly balloon into major battles. Of course, escalating battles will get your teen to talk to you…but certainly not in a good way! Therefore, as you decide which issues are worth battling over, we suggest you consider the following criteria and then discuss your thoughts with your teen and get her input.

- Ask yourself, Is this a character issue, or simply a matter of personal preference? If it boils down to personal preferences, it is rarely worth battling over. If your teen wants to get her ear pierced, that's one thing. But if she wants to stay out all night, that's another. If you allow everything to become a battle, she will soon turn a deaf ear—even on big issues.
- Ask yourself, Is this going to matter a year from now? One month from now? Spilled milk on the living room carpeting is one thing, but sneaking liquor into the house is quite another.
- Are you saying no out of conviction or unreasonable fear? Healthy fear is a good thing—you don't want your sixteen-year-old out on the streets at 2 A.M. However, she is probably safe going with a group of kids to a late movie.
- Are you a control freak? If you are, every issue will loom large. So control your urges to control just for the sake of being controlling.

- Are you a perfectionist? Perfectionists would often rather be right than be happy, and this mind-set will set up a lot of battles that just aren't worth fighting over. Would you rather be right than have your teen talk to you? Absolutely not.
- Develop the habit of saying yes whenever possible. This builds credibility in your teen's eyes and makes her more receptive when you do need to say no.
- Don't make battle decisions when you're tired.
- Is this something your teen repeatedly asks about? If so, this request may be more important to her than you realize. Get to the root of why she wants to do what she repeatedly asks to do, and then make your judgment. Say, "Can you tell me why this is so important to you?"
- Gather the facts before making a decision.
- Stay calm. If you need more facts, tell her you'll reconsider her request when she gets you those facts. Don't be afraid to call other parents to get needed information.
- Don't jump the gun or fly off the handle at the first hint of a dispute.
- Remember that it's fine to say, "I need time to think about this," or "I want to talk to your father about this before I make a decision."
- Remember that it's okay to say no. Say it firmly and with authority.
- Keep in mind that your teen may not be happy with your decision and may try to make you feel guilty. Say, "I realize you're upset, and I'm sorry that you are, but my decision remains the same."
- Express high regard for your teen's feelings. For instance: "I know how much your heart was set on doing this, but right now Dad and I feel it's unwise for you to do such and so."
- If you feel something is a battle and your mate doesn't, you're in a *lose-lose* situation. Be sure to present a united front, so that your teen doesn't zero in on your conflict and try to play one parent against the other.
- Don't withdraw emotionally in the midst of battle. Your teen

may give you the cold shoulder, but you need to remain supportive and engaged.

- Assure your teen of your love for her. This is especially important in the heat of battle.
- If you blow it, apologize. Your teen will respect you all the more for it.

In his book *Parenting Isn't for Cowards*, James Dobson explains the "Loosen and Tighten Principle." When our children become teenagers, he says, we should "loosen [our] grip on the things that don't have any lasting significance and tighten [our] grip on the things that do."[11]

In other words, give most of your attention to what is truly important in life. Don't major on the minors, so to speak. Dobson says, "Don't throw away your friendship over behavior that has no moral significance"[12]

Since parenting teens requires lots of energy, make sure yours is well spent. Focus on the big issues, not the small ones. Don't make mountains out of molehills. Also keep in mind that if everything looks like a mountain, it may be time to step back and readjust your perspective.

Make mountains out of mountains—and leave the molehills alone!

⌒≈⌒

Bottom Line: As Thomas Jefferson once said, "In matters of principle, stand like a rock. In matters of taste, swim with the current."

CHAPTER SEVENTEEN

IF YOU'RE OPEN, I'M OPEN

Are You Available?

My parents make time for me.
Some of my friends' parents give them money instead of time.
I'd lots rather have their time.

STEVE, 17

Because my (Connie) daughters' high school had what's called "modular scheduling," each week they usually had a free period or two. When they were seniors, they discovered they both were "open" during the same mods on Wednesday mornings. Since I knew that the girls would soon be heading off to college, early in the school year I said, "Girls, if you're open, I'm open." In other words, if they were free and wanted to spend that time with me, I'd make being available to them my highest priority.

So on most Wednesday mornings you could have found us sipping hot beverages and maybe splitting a bagel at the little coffee shop across the street from their high school—talking about whatever was going on in their lives at the time.

Although you probably don't have a work-at-home flex-schedule like mine that allows for Wednesday morning coffee dates, you may be able to identify other set times in the week for spending dedicated time with your teen. How about starting a routine of taking Saturday morning walks together? Or dinner dates with your teen once a month? Or reading the Sunday paper together on the front porch?

However, making time to talk with your teen will usually be an unscheduled event. This is because teens are renowned for wanting to talk at the most unusual times—like early in the mornings when we're trying to get everyone out the door. Or late at night when we're tired. Or in the middle of the afternoon when we're trying to get six things done at once. Since their readiness to talk and our readiness to listen rarely coincide naturally, meaningful conversations often require a quick and unexpected parental leap into the *stop-and-listen* mode.

So if you want to know what's going on in their lives, you'll probably be the one doing the schedule-tweaking most of the time. Why? Because teens tend to share their hearts spontaneously—when the mood hits, so to speak. But once that mood passes, their attention has moved elsewhere. So, as soon as you sense they're ready to talk, stop what you're doing and listen to them—in other words, be open.

Recently, there was a panel of teens who talked about what parents could do to encourage communication. The room was packed out with parents—every parent in that room wanted to know how to better relate to his or her kids. Surprisingly, one kid after another said, "Make yourself available to us. If we want to talk, stop whatever you're doing (within reason) and talk to us." Their message came in loud and clear: Don't let opportunities to talk to your kids pass you by!

One teenager girl we know recently told us: "We don't always feel like talking to our parents. We often prefer talking to our friends instead. So if your teen is open to talking, do whatever you can to talk to her right then. You may be tired or trying to cook dinner or something. It doesn't matter. Stop what you're doing and give her your attention. And when you give us your attention, give it to us 100 percent. If we sense that you're listening with your ears only, but your heart isn't really into it or that you really don't care all that much about what we're trying to tell you about, we'll stop talking. If you let the opportunity pass, it may be a long time before it comes back again. Plus, you'll probably never know what we had on our minds at that particular time. Once the opportunity passes, it's gone."

As you rearrange your priorities so you can be available when your teen begins to open up to you, keep in mind that the teen years fly by and will be gone before you know it.

Also, remember that keeping communication alive during her teen years is the best bridge to having open communication with her when she is an adult.

❧

Bottom Line: Strike while the iron is hot!

CHAPTER EIGHTEEN

TO SPOIL OR NOT TO SPOIL
Can't Buy Me Love

*My parents always said they loved us too much to spoil us.
I'm glad they raised us like they did. They were right—spoiling
doesn't equal love, but raising an appreciative kid does.*

JASON, 19

Because parents today tend to have more discretionary income, spoiling their children has become a huge temptation. Simply put, as part of an affluent society, we can afford to spoil our children. While spoiling our kids may seem noble on the surface, it won't bode anyone well later in life—the child or the parents.

Many parents spoil their children in an effort to buy their love and friendship. But this doesn't work. Instead, the teen often loses respect for the parent. Because a spoiled child generally expects much and appreciates little, the parent/child relationship is usually damaged, rather than strengthened, by spoiling.

One set of parents—who are also dear friends of ours—got caught up in spoiling their children and later regretted it. Describing their dilemma, they said, "Even though our intentions were good, we had no idea that our approach would create such an 'I deserve it' attitude. Frankly, our kids have become children that are not all that pleasant to be around."

While some parents try to befriend their kids by spoiling them, others do it because they are trying to make their children's lives as easy as possible. Family dynamics and negative effects that are common to many families with spoiled children include:

- *Expectations of the teen are very low.* She is only expected to do the simplest of chores around the house, and even those are open to discussion. Many times she forgets to do them or does not do them well. She is seldom required to improve the quality or quantity of her efforts. Instead, the parent steps in and takes over—making excuses for the child. She quickly learns how to work the system to her advantage, playing one parent against the other if one is less adamant.

The child is the one who really misses out here. For one thing, research shows that chores build a teen's self-esteem and instills a sense of responsibility. Plus, doing chores is a wonderful way for teens to contribute to the family unit—to be a giver and not just a taker. A life of ease now *does not* translate into responsible and caring adults who are prepared for the challenges of life later.

- *Parents overstock their kids with items they want but do not need.* We can't stress enough the importance of teaching your teen the difference between a *want* and a need. For example, a new pair of tennis shoes may indeed be a need, but a $150 pair is definitely a want.

- *Parents invest in all sorts of electronic gadgets and machines that keep their teens entertained for hours—and then these same parents wonder why their teens don't take time to talk to them.* Teens that are too *plugged in* and entertained don't have time to think deeply and talk openly. This life of entertainment paves the way for kids to be *plugged out* relationally and *plugged into* a lot of impulse buying and debt later in life.

- *The parents excessively cater to the teen.* For example, if Joe is hungry for ice cream at midnight, Dad heads to the grocery store right away. And on those rare occasions when Dad tells Joe to find something to eat that's already in the pantry or fridge, Mom twists Dad's arm to go to the store or heads there herself.

In either case, Dad's authority in the home is being eroded. Since God's design for families is for Dad to be the leader in the home, eroding this position of leadership circumvents God's plan for the family as a whole and for its individual members. When this occurs, you are effectively teaching your teen how to "beat the system" in regards to authority, limits, and rules.

One of the best ways to ruin a child is to allow her to think your home is the Ritz-Carlton and that she is the guest in residence. A child who carries this self-centered "I deserve it" mentality into adulthood is in for a rude awakening. Others won't find this trait charming in the least.

Delayed gratification is a valuable lesson that every child should learn. Kids who are taught this generally become adults who are willing to work hard for long-term goals and not throw in the towel when the chips are down or frustration hits.

Spoiling Handicaps the Child

Are you spoiling your child? Listed below is a short overview of how a spoiled child actually ends up being handicapped later in life. If something in the pit of your stomach tells you that your child is headed in this direction, it's time for a course correction.

- *She will grow up thinking the world revolves around her.* Although it may appear that way while she is in your home, she'll soon discover that the rest of the world—particularly her teachers and, later on, her employers—don't agree with this undeserved assessment of her importance.
- *She learns to get by with as little effort as possible.* Typically, when a child is spoiled, *excellence* is not a word that is familiar to her.
- *She never quite learns that no means "no."* (We'll discuss this further in the next chapter).
- *Studies show that she is at risk for depression and will tend to lack strong character.*

Today's parents often try very hard to create a perfect little world—devoid of pain, hardship, and disappointment—in which they think their child will thrive. Somehow we have forgotten the invaluable lessons that can only be learned through facing challenges, sometimes overcoming them and sometimes not. We forget how pain teaches us to appreciate the good times; hardships remind us of all we have to be thankful for; life's bumps are often our springboards to perseverance and strength of character; and disappointment forces us to get back up, wipe ourselves off, and try again. These are some of life's most powerful lessons—without them, we are handicapped.

When you are there to weather the storms with your child while she is living under your roof, you are preparing her for the larger storms she will face later—when she is out on her own. Over time she'll grow to appreciate how you cared enough to let her learn to roll with the punches and make do with what she already has. And as she talks to you and asks your advice about what is on her heart as she faces challenges and obstacles that occur naturally, you will be giving her tools for coping with the ups and downs she will face later in life.

Which is more important: fulfilling her whims of the moment and demands for more entertainment and ease or giving her the tools that will last for a lifetime?

~≈~

Bottom Line: If you give your child a silver platter, make sure what you place on it is worth serving.

CHAPTER NINETEEN

SAYING NO
AND MEANING IT

How to Say No Correctly

*Thanks, Mom and Dad, for not letting me do things with
people you don't know. I don't always say this, but
I appreciate your protection.*

JODI, 16

⁓

"Good" conversations with our teens—the kind that parents long to
have with their teens—are not riddled with conflict, frustration, and
anger. But how do we get there? Believe it or not, learning to say no
convincingly and with authority will alleviate—and often circum-
vent—tension between you and your teen.

We don't do our teen any favors when he thinks our no may
mean "maybe"! Because all teens test the waters to see if we're still
sticking to our guns, staying committed to consistency is vital.

Here are a few tried and true tips for evading conflict by making
sure your no really means "no."

- Never give a "no" answer flippantly. First, carefully consider the
  facts. Then ask yourself, "Do I really feel strongly about this?"
- Don't say no just because you're tired or angry. Too often, parents say no when they are too tired to consider the matter rea-
  sonably, but then change their minds later. When haphazard
  and changeable decisions are the norm, parents are saying that
  their first word is not their final one. If you value your first
  word, so will he.
- When no is your first and final answer, say it calmly and with
  authority. Remain composed even if he becomes upset.

83

Calmness, however, should not leave the decision open for discussion.

- Don't be apologetic. After all, why would you feel bad about making a decision after you have carefully considered the facts to determine what is in the best interest of your child and everyone else concerned? Sure, tell him how much you care about his sadness ("I know you had your heart set on this, and I'm so sorry you're disappointed"), but don't apologize for saying no.

   If he thinks you doubt your decision, he will assume there is still room for negotiation. But if he sees that you are convinced you made the correct decision, he will be more convinced of your sound judgment himself.

- Don't allow your teen to heap guilt on you. Don't yield to his pressure, whining, or begging, and let him know there will be consequences for wielding manipulative tactics.

- Explain why. If you can't explain why, you probably haven't thought the facts through thoroughly enough. Therefore, rethink your position before giving your answer. Even if he doesn't agree with you, a "no" answer will be easier for him to accept if he hears your reasoning.

- Once you've explained why, don't feel you need to defend your decision over and over again if he continues to challenge it. For example, if you have said, "Because Dad's been out of town all week, we think we need some family time. Derrik can spend the night next weekend instead." If your teen asks why family time can't wait for another day, simply say, "I've told you why Derrik cannot spend the night here tonight, and I'm not going to explain it again. If you keep pushing this issue, Derrik won't be spending the night next weekend either."

- Don't say no but then change your mind when bending your decision would make life a little easier for you. For example, if your son isn't allowed to drive for a week, don't bend the rules so he can run to the grocery store for you.

If your no hasn't meant "no" in the past, explain to your teen that you've been doing some thinking lately and have decided some changes in that department are needed. Assure him that your new, long-term commitment to consistency will benefit the whole family—otherwise he'll figure that he's going to be losing out while you're gaining from the change.

If you feel the least bit intimidated or guilty about saying no, practice what you're going to say beforehand. Your rehearsal may sound something like this:

- "I've decided my answer is no. I like to say yes whenever I can, but I am convinced that I need to say no in this case."
- "I've thought a lot about what we discussed the other night, and my answer is no."
- "I understand your reasoning, but I don't agree with you."
- "After you have more driving experience, you can use the other car."
- "We've already talked about this, and my final answer is no."

Finally, don't forget that it is not your duty to get your teen to agree with you or to convince him that you're right. Nor is it your job to make sure he doesn't get angry or upset about your decisions. Your job is to be the best parent you can possibly be—and that doesn't mean saying yes to his every request. When your child sees that *you* respect your own word, *he* will respect it too. This consistency will cause him to respect the words of others as well. He will carry into the world what he learns at your feet.

When your no is really no and your first word means exactly what you said, your child's respect for you will grow. This will also cause your teen's own self-respect to increase. This win-win situation will strengthen your relationship with your teen and increase "good" communication with him.

~

Bottom Line: Remember, you're the parent!

CHAPTER TWENTY

SAY YES AS OFTEN AS POSSIBLE

The Deaf-Ear Antidote

*My parents are so cool. They don't nitpick
about all the small stuff like some of my buddies' parents do.
Man, those parents are exhausting.*

CYRIL, 15

❧

Saying yes as much as possible is one of the most basic principles of parenting. Your tendency will be to say no to almost everything if you're overprotective, overly controlling, or unreasonably fearful of all that is out there that may stumble your child. Being around someone who constantly says no (remember when your two-year-old went through that phase?) is exhausting, frustrating, and no fun! This is particularly true for teens that are by nature eager to spread their wings a bit and see if they can "fly" apart from Mom and Dad.

Saying yes to your teen as much as possible communicates a number of things:

- You trust her.
- You've not forgotten what it's like to be a teenager.
- You enjoy seeing her have fun and getting to do new things.
- You have confidence in her decision-making abilities.
- When you say no, it's for a reason other than just hearing yourself talk.
- You don't see controlling her life as the chief purpose for your existence.
- You feel she's responsible enough to do what she's asking to do.

Saying yes to your teen as often as possible takes the sting out of the times when you'll have to say no. It lets your teen know that you'll seriously consider her request and won't just say no out of habit or unnecessary fear. And because she's seen your pattern of saying yes whenever possible, she'll eventually piece together the knowledge that when you do say no, it's for a good reason—even if she can't connect the dots to your decision.

If you can't say yes in the short term, say it for the long term whenever it's reasonable to do so. For example:

Remember a few chapters ago when we talked about the teen boy asking his dad to run to the store at midnight to buy a certain kind of ice cream? Instead of simply saying, "No, I am not going to the store at midnight to buy you ice cream," he might say, "I'm not going to the store now. It's much too late and there's plenty of other food to eat in the house, but if you remind me about this tomorrow, I'll drive you to the store so you get some then."

Using this approach, Dad says no in the short term, but the boy knows that he will be eating his favorite ice cream tomorrow—if he still wants it then! This long-term approach to saying yes helps your teen see that you appreciate his wishes and advocate for his happiness, even though he doesn't always instantly get what he wants.

When it comes to saying yes and no, you and your spouse will have many gray areas to discuss. Many times what I (Connie) hold tightly to, Wes doesn't; and what he feels firmly about, I tend to be looser on! Isn't that the way it so often goes? But a little communication, a lot of compromise, and a whole bunch of prayer go a long way in knowing what to do. If it's a huge deal to Wes, I don't ask him to compromise, and he does the same for me. In those instances we back each other up. In the other instances we reach a compromise by each giving in a little to the other's wishes. I used to get annoyed with our little differences. But over the years I've learned to appreciate how Wes balances me out in areas where I tend to be too rigid...and I know our girls appreciate this balance too!

Rather than fixating on your differences and allowing them to drive you crazy—as well as drive a wedge between you and your spouse—thank God for the way He's chosen to use your marriage to balance each of your perspectives.

If you're a first-time parent of a teen, you will probably tend to think all issues are major, and if you're not careful, you'll end up saying no to practically everything except "Can I brush my teeth three times a day?" This tendency in first-timers is highlighted by the fact that older siblings usually end up lamenting about how much easier the younger ones have it later. By the time the younger ones are teens, Mom and Dad are far more acute in recognizing what's a big deal and what isn't. To this day, my (Connie) oldest sister still complains: "I had to be in at 9:30 on my first date...." (I just laugh because I know my parents were a lot more reasonable by the time my turn came around!)

Regardless of whether you're a first-timer or not, the principle is still the same: Say yes whenever it's reasonable to do so. But before giving your teen a yes answer, be sure that you and your spouse agree on how you will respond. Otherwise, your teen may look for ways to play one parent against another—and that kind of parent hopping should always result in a firm no.

≈

Bottom line: Yes is music to a teen's ear...and makes an occasional no an easier sound to hear.

CHAPTER TWENTY-ONE

THE MYTH
OF QUALITY TIME

Wake up and Smell the Coffee!

*The one thing my parents are really doing right is
they always make sure we spend time together as a family,
eating dinner together and being involved in each other's lives.*
RACHEL, 15

❈

"Sixteen hundred people belong to the International Flat Earth Research Society of America. Their president, Charles K. Johnson, says he's been a flat-earther all his life. 'When I saw the globe in grade school, I didn't accept it then, and I don't accept it now.'"[13]

Unbelievable! Even though science, geography, astronomy, space travel, photographs, and every other aspect associated with the study of earth points to the fact that the earth is round, some people still embrace the myth that the earth is flat. Such thinking goes against logic. It's enough to make a person want to scream, "Wake up and smell the coffee!"

There is also a parenting myth that makes us want to scream. That myth is called *quality time.* Now don't get us wrong, quality time is attainable with teenagers. However, the futility of how to attain it is what drives us nuts. Thinking they can somehow conjure it up or will it into existence, parents insist, "Today we're going to spend quality time with Jake." This is a myth because quality time is seldom a planned event.

So what is quality time? It's a natural by-product of quantity time. It just sort of happens in the midst of spending large amounts of time with our teen. It frequently occurs by accident, often when we least expect it:

- While playing basketball in the driveway with your son, he asks you a question about dating and suddenly...quality time happens.
- Taking a coffee break during Christmas shopping with your daughter gives her an opportunity to ask your opinion on a career path...quality time.
- Playing a board game with your son and a few of his buddies turns into a conversation about politics...quality time.
- Regularly getting up early to go for a jog with your daughter allows her to raise an issue that has been racing around in her mind for months...quality time.
- After a church service, your teen asks spiritually significant questions...quality time.

Do you want *quality* time to happen? Then don't force it. Instead, let it happen naturally by spending *quantity* time with your teen. Do hobbies together. Play games. Exercise. Go to a flick and then out for coffee. Wash the car. Take a swim. Fathers, do daddy dates. Moms, try ladies' nights out. Almost anything will work as long as you slow down and spend time with your teen.

A word of caution: Don't try to cram a hidden agenda down your kid's throat in the name of quality time, like a friend of ours did. The words of his fourteen-year-old daughter say it far better than we can: "I wish my dad was interested in me more than he was interested in my ability to be a great basketball player. I think it's good that he supports me, but all he ever wants to talk about is how I can get better. And if we go anywhere, it's a college basketball game or the high school play-offs. It always has to do with basketball. All of his time with me revolves around basketball. That's fine and all, but sometimes I wish some of our time just revolved around me, without the basketball stuff. Sometimes I feel like he loves how I play more than he loves me."

So remember three things:

1. No hidden agendas.
2. No matter how creative or mundane, the activity itself isn't what produces quality time. Since quality time is a by-product of quantity time, the way to plan for it is to spend extended

time with your teen. What's more, quality time usually happens accidentally, so be sure to seize the moment when it presents itself.

3. Finally, since quality time only happens in the midst of mutual trust, respect, and love, keep making regular deposits into your teen's life.

∾

Bottom Line: When it comes to time, quality is usually hidden in the quantity.

CHAPTER TWENTY-TWO

SAY IT AND SPRAY IT

Know Your Teen's Love Language

*I've learned that love looks different on the outside from
person to person, but it all feels the same on the inside.*
TONYA, 18

~≈~

Understanding the different ways each of you gives and receives love is
one of the quickest and most profound ways to effect positive change
in your relationship with your teenager. Dr. Gary Chapman wrote
about this concept in his bestselling book *The Five Love Languages* and
in his follow-up book *The Five Love Languages of Teenagers.* We highly
recommend both books.

Dr. Chapman explains that each of us speaks one of five primary
"love languages." These include: words of affirmation, quality time,
gifts, acts of service, and physical touching. The titles are fairly self-
explanatory, but here's a quick overview of each love language:

Words of affirmation. These children thrive on being verbally
affirmed. When you compliment them or remark about what a wonderful job they did, they blossom. Not surprisingly, if you rain criticism on their parades, they shrivel and withdraw. This is how I (Kent)
felt in elementary school. One of my primary love languages is words
of affirmation. But because of my academic struggles, I didn't hear
many compliments from teachers. And because of my nerdiness, I felt
pretty unaccepted by my peers. However, my parents evidently recognized my need for affirmation. Without their telling me I was valuable, I would have been a pretty empty kid.

Quality time. These kids enjoy "just hanging out" with others.
One of my (Connie) daughters is this way. She loves going to the bagel
shop with me and just talking. It's not surprising that going to the

movies isn't ranked high on her list of favorite things to do. Why? Because at the movies you just sit…you don't share your hearts with each another.

Because it takes a greater investment of time, this language is more difficult to speak than some of the others. If quality time isn't your love language, spending time with your teen won't come naturally, and you will need to pencil it in on your calendar. If you discover that hanging out with you is one of your teen's love languages, your time spent with her will be speaking volumes of love to her.

Gifts. Teens with this language are natural gift-givers. My (Connie) youngest daughter falls into this group. This past Christmas I asked our family how they would feel if we adopted a family and gave gifts to them instead of exchanging gifts with each other (obviously, gifts isn't my love language!). When my daughter balked at this idea, I thought, *Where's her spirit of generosity? Doesn't she realize how much we have and how little others do?* About this time she said, "Mom, I don't care if I get any gifts, but can I please buy gifts for you, Daddy, and Sissies? I just love buying for everyone." From her tender comment, I was able to assess that her love language is gifts. From now on, I will keep her love language in mind when I am looking for ways to express my love to her and to provide opportunities for her to express her love to us.

A couple of mental notes about the language of gifts:

- If you're giving something to your teen for services rendered, that's not a bona-fide gift. A gift is something freely given for no apparent reason—other than to say "I love you."
- Don't tie a gift to a bribe like: "I've been asking you to rake the leaves. If you get them raked, I'll buy you that new CD you want."
- Dr. Chapman mentions the importance of giving gifts ceremoniously. Wrap your gift in bright paper and give it to your teen at the dinner table or in front of the entire family. Make it a big deal: "Because we love you so much and appreciate the kind of person you are, we wanted to give you this." Most parents make the mistake of taking their teen to the mall, buying

her what she wants, and leaving it at that. This communicates little emotional love and creates what Dr. Chapman calls an "entitlement" mentality in your teen. But when you wrap it up, talk it up, and then present it with a grand flourish…then it becomes a gift!

- Keep in mind that gifts don't have to be expensive or even purchased. They can be something as simple as baking her favorite pie for no apparent reason or surprising her with a favorite meal.
- Finally, never give gifts as a replacement for love. Perhaps you are overtaxed at work, travel frequently, and rush to get everything done each day because you're a single parent. Whatever your unique situation may be, don't make the mistake of thinking a gift can replace you…it can't.

Acts of service. A ray of sunshine exists in the homes that are graced with these gifted people! They enjoy doing things for others and are especially appreciative when others do various things for them—picking up their dry cleaning, stocking the refrigerator, taking their car to get it washed.

Here are some helpful tips about the teen whose love language is acts of service:

- Don't make your teen feel like she's imposing when she asks you to help her with something.
- Use your acts of service to teach your teen lifetime skills. For example, cooking supper for her is indeed an act of service, but teaching her to cook her own supper is even better.
- Don't worry that you're creating a dependent child. Generally, do acts of service for your teens that they are unable to do for themselves. When they are young, you wash their clothes for them; when they become teens, you teach them how to wash the clothes. This does not mean that you never do your teen's laundry. But it does mean that you will not always do it for her. First you model, then you guide your teen toward independent actions and maturity.[14]

Physical touch. These folks are the huggers and embracers. They can't sit next to a loved one without touching them. I (Kent) can attest to this since I'm a toucher. I naturally hug and kiss my kids the moment I see them. It's the way I speak love.

Once your child becomes a teen, the rules change a bit. They probably won't like being embraced in front of their peers. To determine if she's open to the love language of touch at any given moment, you'll need to gauge your teen's mood. As Dr. Chapman notes, "If your teenager's primary love language in childhood was physical touch, the love language will not change during the adolescent years. However, the dialect in which you speak that language must change if you want the teenager to feel loved."[15]

A few closing thoughts to aid you in discerning your teen's love language:

- Ask her who in her life makes her feel special. When she gives you an answer, ask her what that person does to make her feel that way.
- Ask, "If you wanted to show someone that you really cared for her, what would you do?"
- Observe how your teen interacts with peers. What does she do to make them feel special? This will not only clue you in to her love language, but it will also provide hints about how you can better communicate with her in general.
- Tune into your teen's complaints. Her complaints serve as snapshots of what speaks love to her.
- Listen to your teen's requests. What a person requests is a tremendous indicator of her primary love language.

❧

Bottom Line. Become bilingual—learn to fluently speak both your love language and your teen's.

CHAPTER TWENTY-THREE

GET A LIFE!

Is Your Teen Claustrophobic?

*Mom and Dad, I love you...but sometimes I just need you to
leave me alone for a while.*
HEATHER, 17

After surveying hundreds of teens, we were most surprised by this finding: Many teens don't want to be such a huge focus of their parents' lives.

They do want to feel important, be loved, and know their parents care about them. But, in a nutshell, they don't like it when their parents' lives are consumed with theirs. This complaint seems to pinpoint moms more than dads. When we conducted research for this book, one teen told us, "My mom doesn't have a life outside of mine," he said. "She wants to be included in everything I do; and if she's not, she's hurt. She's constantly asking me questions about what I'm going to do next, who I'm going to do it with, where I'm going to go, and on and on. She's always, like, so there. I'm almost eighteen and would love a little room to breathe, but I'm not sure she's ever going to give me that until I'm out of the house completely. I know that this sounds like a 'good' problem to have, and I'm glad she cares about me, but she drives me crazy with her constant questions and willingness to be involved in my life. I think it would be much better for all of us if she found some friends her own age to hang out with."

The kid is right! It's not healthy for your life to completely revolve around your child's. In other words, get a life! Statistics show that if a woman has just one special friend, her other relationships are healthier. Why? She isn't expecting the husband—or in this case, the teen—to meet all of her needs and make her feel complete and fulfilled. Like the teen pointed out in our example, people in every kind of relationship need room to breathe.

Of course it's fine to ask your teen where he's going to be, who he'll be with, and what time he'll be home, but don't insist that he tell you about everything in his life. Silence is golden, and so is privacy. Allow your teen his privacy. Don't take it personally if he doesn't include you in every aspect of his life. This is normal, even healthy.

Even when you're seeking only to learn what's going on in his life, digging around to get all the nitty-gritty details of your teen's everyday life tells him that you don't trust him. Slowly, he will grow to resent your meddling—and ultimately, he will resent you too. Plus, sometimes when trustworthy kids think their parents don't trust them, they give up. The result? Weak communication and bad behavior problems!

It's been said before that a child will frequently raise or lower himself to his parents' expectations of him. Why not let him know that until proven otherwise, you trust him to make wise decisions? The more your teen sees evidence that you trust him, the more he'll want to live up to those expectations. Then, in his efforts to make good choices, he will invite your input. Remember, however, that pressing him for details before he's ready to share them is like issuing an invitation for him to clam up.

And so we now come back to the idea of getting your own life. Your son will see your constant intrusion as an indicator that you don't trust him—even when it's really because you are trying to keep him at the center of your universe. As his resentment builds, he will withdraw from you, and your communication with him will deteriorate. Then, rather than coming to you for help, he will run from talking to you and may even do the very opposite of what he thinks you would suggest he do.

The solution: Take a hard and honest look at the real motives behind why you want to be so wrapped up in your teen's life. Maybe it's not so much that you don't trust him as it is that you've wrapped your happiness quotient around having all of your emotional needs met through your child.

Bottom Line: Get a life, and let your teen have his!

CHAPTER TWENTY-FOUR

PLAY FAIR

What Not to Say

Hypocrisy, just pure hypocrisy.
It upsets me when my parents are so hypocritical.
MARVIN, 17

❧

Do you remember teaching your son or daughter to play fairly? We do! Both of us have twin girls, so teaching fairness early on was essential for maintaining peace in our households. We always had an eye on whose turn it was to answer the phone, get the mail, play with a favorite doll, or use the computer.

But the concept of fairness usually becomes a bit more challenging for parents after their kids become teenagers. While we may have done a pretty good job of helping our kids juggle a myriad of activities when they were younger, we suddenly find it hard to play fairly with our teens ourselves. In fact, we all probably need a refresher course on how to communicate with them fairly.

To help us play—or communicate—more fairly with our teens, here are a number of "what *not* to say" tips.

SACRED PARENT SAYINGS

Michael Ross, in his book *How to Speak Alien,* describes "sacred parent sayings" that each generation of parents seems to pass down to the next. We all hated our parents using these sayings, but for some reason we carry on this awful tradition of passing them down to our children.

As you read the sayings listed below, reflect on whether any of these common phrases are in your own speech patterns. We have added a few of our own to Ross's list of sayings.

- "As long as you're living under my roof, you'll do exactly as I say. End of discussion!"
- "Do you actually think you are leaving the house wearing that?"
- "This is going to hurt me more than it's going to hurt you."
- "If only you acted more like your sister."
- "It's not that I don't trust you; I just don't trust your choice of friends."
- "Someday when you're older you'll understand."
- "Clean your room—it looks like a pigsty!"
- "I don't like your attitude. Do you want to be grounded for life?"
- "Would you jump off a bridge if your friends did?"
- "Do I look like I'm made out of money?"[16]

Here are some other sayings (we compiled) that may sound familiar:

- "In my day…"
- "Shut your mouth. Do you understand me? (pause) Answer me!" (This is one of the all-time, ridiculous contradictions.)
- "Who do you think you are that you can talk to me in that tone of voice?"
- "I'm so sick and tired…." (Bill Cosby said the worst spanking he ever received was when his dad said, "I'm so sick…" and Bill chimed in with "and tired".)
- "Wipe that look off your face."
- "Do you think your socks will just pick themselves up off the floor?"

Before continuing the tradition of repeating and, ultimately, passing down a "sacred parent saying," shouldn't we ask ourselves what this canned phrase will accomplish? Will this phrase blossom—or will it bust—conversation with my child?

THE GUNNYSACK

What we call the "gunnysack" is even more dim-witted than the "sacred parent sayings." When we allow old, unresolved issues to make their way into heated discussions about new issues, we have just emptied our gunnysacks. How fair is this? If we hold on to our anger and disappointment over situations that happened with our teens in the past and then pour them out later when we are addressing a completely different situation, we frustrate and confuse our teens. The end result? Their defenses go up—and they dump all their own gunnysack issues out onto the table too.

So how do we avoid this communication buster? By dealing with conflicts or concerns right away and then letting go of the emotions we have attached to them—permanently.

Keep your gunnysack as empty as possible and deal only with the issues at hand.

COUNT TO TEN

Also, don't respond in anger. Obviously, this is much easier said than done. But to play fairly, be sure you don't

- speak without thinking. The old saying "count to ten" gives us a chance to figure out why we're angry and if we're overreacting.
- speak without listening. Do you like being interrupted? Of course not. Then how can we expect teens not to get irritated when we interrupt them? *Learn to use your mute button.*
- speak with volume control.

When our children are young, we teach them to play fairly with others. When they are teens, we teach them to communicate fairly by doing so ourselves.

⎯⎯⎯

Bottom Line: Don't turn kids off by speaking unfairly.

CHAPTER TWENTY-FIVE

CHANGING THE RULES

How to Ask Questions That Get Responses

*I think my parents want to talk to me;
they just don't know what to say.*
KYLIE, 15

❧

Which would you prefer: Authentic conversation *with* your teen? Or dead-on-arrival, resentful replies *from* him?

Certainly, like any other parent, you want to strengthen your relationship with your child through honest and genuine communication. While no parent seeks to talk at their child and have him retort with begrudged replies, all too many parent/teen conversations end up getting short-circuited within the first sentence or two.

Here are some strategies that pave the way to open-hearted discussions.

- *Don't* just ask "yes" or "no" questions. Questions that start with "Do you think...?" or "Is that...?" usually solicit a one-word opinion instead of generating a discussion.
- *Do* ask "why" questions like "Why do you think that?" or "Why do you want to go to the party?" "Why" questions lead teens to reason through and articulate their responses. Plus, if asked with sincerity, "why" questions keep dialogue from becoming overly emotional.
- *Don't* just ask for facts. Getting facts is great, but don't you want to engage your teen's mind and heart?
- *Do* ask about feelings. Questions about feelings encourage teens to share on a more personal level. This promotes intimacy and depth in the parent-child relationship. When feelings are shared, more trust is built.

- *Don't* assume. This is a basic communication hurdle that most parents trip on often. Since assumptions shut down communication, what good is a question like "I know what you are thinking, but why did you do such a thing?" By telling our teen that we know what he is thinking, we are saying that we have already formed our opinion about how we are going to respond. So why should he try to explain?

- *Do* show that you care. A slight methodological change in the above approach can make a significant difference. Instead of starting out with "I know what you are thinking…," try saying, "I care about you, so tell me why…." *Genuine care encourages authentic response.*

- *Don't* interrogate. You're a parent, not a police officer. Interrogations will shut your teen down faster than you can click on a flashlight.

- *Do* ask direct questions. This approach avoids the extremes of interrogation on the one hand or beating around the bush on the other. Plus, it gets you right to the heart of a matter. Obviously, one must learn how and when to ask such questions. Without sensitivity, direct questions can be disastrous. Yet when asked sincerely and lovingly, they take discussion to a deeper level.

- *Don't* focus on knowing everything. When a discussion moves to a debate or dispute, don't be overly concerned about whether you have all the answers. No parent has all the answers. Instead, focus more on the manner in which you respond. Is your manner and content honest and sincere? Are you communicating how much you value your teen and his input? Sure, you want to be right, but isn't responding in the correct manner just as important?

Keep in mind that our teens need us to help them develop their reasoning and communication skills. If they can only parrot the opinions we have forced upon them and if they do not know why they believe what they think they believe, they will be standing on shaky ground when hard circumstances challenge their values later.

- *Do* seek opinions. Is there any better way to connect with and understand your teen than to hear firsthand what he or she is thinking? While you might not always like what you hear, at least you are discovering what is going on inside of him. This gives you the opportunity to constructively challenge him! So remember, when dealing with opinions, it is your questions— and not your answers—that make for good conversation.
- *Don't* overexaggerate. "You *always* act that way!" "You *never* do what I ask." These responses are as counterproductive as making assumptions. They sound accusing and cause a teenager to engage his defense systems.
- *Do* use "I" statements. Although you don't want to overexaggerate, you also don't want to wimp out and never speak the truth. Therefore, raise a concern candidly with statements like "I feel…" or "I don't understand…." Also, for most confrontational conversations, start by emphasizing your desires with "I" statements.

Although asking good questions is not overwhelmingly important for parenting small children, it's vital in parenting teenagers. Asking good questions keeps us from one-sided lectures where we do all of the talking and our teens do all of the ignoring. Inviting our teens to process and communicate their thoughts will empower and prepare them to respond appropriately to challenging situations that occur outside of the home and later in life.

Asking good questions accomplishes more than coming up with correct answers.

⤙

Bottom Line: Ask away—in the right way!

CHAPTER TWENTY-SIX

ANGER

Yours and Theirs

When your parents get mad at you and scream and holler,
it makes you feel like a worm.
DANIEL, 13

❧

I'll (Connie) never forget the morning I saw a young friend I'd known for years stagger up the stairs of my daughters' school. As the teenager began to ascend the stairs, his head was bent and he tried to hug the wall. Although he was doing his best to remain inconspicuous, a haunting and painful sound escaped his lips—I realized that he was crying. I rushed down the stairs, put my arm around him, and quietly led him to a nearby office.

I assumed that a family member had died, but when Mark began to speak between sobs, I discovered this wasn't the case at all. Describing how his father had just berated him, this teenage boy told me, "He said things he should have never said to me. He was so angry. He said the most hateful things you can imagine—things a kid shouldn't have to hear." As this young man began to cry again, my heart went out to him.

Apparently, Mark's father had lost his temper and spewed forth a vitriol of hurtful words as he hustled and bustled to drop Mark off at school that morning.

If you want your teen to talk to you, there's one thing you'd better get a handle on quickly—your anger. Why? Because teens have no desire to talk to a parent who erupts easily or often. They quickly learn to save their efforts for something that has a greater chance of paying off—like the lottery.

Some years ago I (Kent) learned the importance of this firsthand when my wife Kathy helped me realize how enslaved I was to "reactive anger." When something would tick me off, I'd explode rapidly. Then, after the anger was out of my system, I was fine. Yet the shrapnel left in my wake was devastating. For the sake of my marriage, profession, and kids, I had to get control of this awful habit.

Maybe you've acquired this habit as well. With God's help, you can change destructive patterns into constructive ones. When taking strides to control your anger when you are talking to your teen, consider taking the following steps:

1. *Admit you have a problem.*

   This requires great courage, but when you consider the toll your teen and the rest of your family will continue to pay if you don't, it becomes far easier. Write this phrase down and say it out loud to a trusted friend: "I have a problem with anger. I say and do things that are hurtful to others, especially to those closest to me. I want to change. And with God's help, I will."

2. *Stop trying to do everything in your own strength.*

   Seek counseling. Your emotional health is every bit as important as your physical health.

3. *Devise a plan of attack.*

   Ask your teen and others closest to you to help you realize when you're losing it.

   Walk out of the room when you feel yourself becoming angry, or allow your teen to withdraw from the scene when she senses an explosion is coming.

   Go for a walk when anger begins to boil too close to the surface.

   Count to ten. Or one hundred. Or one thousand. Or as high as it takes for the vein in your neck to no longer jut out past your chin.

   Involve yourself in some form of physical exercise or exertion.

   Take a long shower or bath.

4. *After you are in control of your emotions, approach the person with whom you are angry and discuss the situation.*

Remember, there are two sides to every story. Consider saying, "I felt upset when such and so occurred. Because I love you, I'd like for you to tell me your perspective of what happened, and then I'd like to share mine."

Don't try to put all of the blame for the source of conflict on your teen. Instead, be willing to accept that some of the problem could lie (Gasp!) with you. And by all means, don't try to blame your teen—or anyone else—for your near explosion.

5. *Use "I" statements instead of "you" statements.*

For example, "I feel upset when such and so occurs" instead of "You make me so angry when you act this way."

6. *Don't interrupt.*

Interrupting shows a lack of respect for your teen and will frustrate her. Remember that you're seeking peaceful, honest, and open communication, not a full-scale war. You can give your two cents when the floor is yours.

7. *Don't bring up the past.*

Again, this is overwhelming and puts your teen on the defensive. It also makes her feel shamed. You should be your teen's ally, not her adversary.

8. *Make certain you understand what your teen means.*

If uncertain, ask questions like, "Are you saying…?" This invites your teen to be more specific—without fear of reprisal.

9. *Compromise when possible.*

If neither of you is going to budge, ask your teen for her suggestions on how to arrive at a better compromise in the future. Remind her that it's okay to disagree with you.

10. *End on a positive note.*

Tell your teen how much you respect her efforts to work through the disagreement in a peaceful manner. Share what you've learned in the process. Let her know how much you love her. This will encourage her to work hard at peacefully resolving conflicts in the future. It will also let her know that your love for her is not contingent on her always agreeing with you.

Negative patterns of behavior *can* be broken, including anger. You don't have to remain in bondage to something so hurtful and destructive. If you continue to struggle with an inability to control outbursts of anger, seek professional help. While this problem won't be conquered overnight, you can make tremendous strides by showing your teen that you are sincerely working toward managing your anger. Your humility will speak volumes to your teenager's heart and will cause her to want to speak volumes to you.

If your teen has a problem with anger, discuss strategies with her to help her get a handle on this early in life. Seek counseling if the problem persists. Most of all, keep in mind that your most effective teaching tool is your example of how you handle conflict.

❦

Bottom Line: Trusted and open communication have room to flourish in a home where anger is managed well.

CHAPTER TWENTY-SEVEN

ACCEPTANCE
The Lap of Luxury

My parents let me know that I'm loved unconditionally
and that it's not based on my performance.
JOEL, 16

❧

Our kids need to know they're loved—as is. If they feel loved only when they meet our requirements or fulfill our expectations, they'll feel unworthy and incompetent. This can put in motion a cycle of insecurity, lack of confidence, and low self-esteem, causing them to give up because they think they'll never measure up. Then, if this cycle isn't broken, it will plague them into adulthood.

Accepting your teen for who he is gives him the freedom to become the fabulous person that dwells within him. He's free to risk…to explore new things…to step out of his comfort zone and even fail at times. But if you do nothing but berate or belittle him for his failures, he'll quickly learn to play it safe at all costs, which will greatly inhibit his maturation into adulthood.

I (Kent) grew up with a speech impediment and poor reading skills. When I reached third grade, my teacher asked my mom, "Do you realize your son can't read?" I remember thinking throughout elementary school, "Oh well, I guess I'm dumb." Even worse, I wasn't a popular kid. I was about four feet by four feet (at least in my eyes) and pretty athletically challenged. In summation, I felt I defined "uncoolness." Yet even though I inwardly fought these private struggles, I never felt unloved or unaccepted by my parents. What's more, my grandparents lived up the street from me, and their constant, unconditional love also meant a ton to me. I can only imagine what scars would have surfaced in my life if my parents and grandparents weren't so accepting!

Philip Yancey, in his book *What's So Amazing about Grace?*, shares this powerful story that reminds us of the incredible power of acceptance:

> A young girl grows up on a cherry orchard just above Traverse City, Michigan. Her parents, a bit old-fashioned, tend to overreact to her nose ring, the music she listens to, and the length of her skirts. They ground her a few times, and she seethes inside. "I hate you!" she screams at her father when he knocks on the door of her room after an argument, and that night she acts on a plan she has mentally rehearsed scores of times. She runs away.
>
> She boards a bus for Detroit and falls under the influence of a pimp. She becomes a prostitute and a drug addict. Eventually she's used up, and the pimp throws her out. Sick, cold, and starving, she longs to go home. Three tries at calling her parents connect only with their answering machine. She leaves a message on the final attempt: "Dad, Mom, it's me. I was wondering about maybe coming home. I'm catching a bus up your way, and it'll get there about midnight tomorrow. If you're not there, well, I guess I'll just stay on the bus until it hits Canada."
>
> When the bus finally rolls into the station, its air brakes hissing in protest, the driver announces in a crackly voice over the microphone, "Fifteen minutes, folks. That's all we have here." Fifteen minutes to decide her life. She checks herself in a compact mirror, smoothes her hair, and licks the lipstick off her teeth. She looks at the tobacco stains on her fingertips and wonders if her parents will notice. If they're there.
>
> She walks into the terminal not knowing what to expect. Not one of the thousand scenes that have played out in her mind prepares her for what she sees. There, in the concrete-walls-and-plastic-chairs bus terminal in Traverse City, Michigan, stands a group of forty brothers and sisters and great-aunts and uncles and cousins and a grandmother and

great-grandmother to boot. They're all wearing goofy party hats and blowing noise makers, and taped across the entire wall of the terminal is a computer-generated banner that reads "Welcome home!"

Out of the crowd of well-wishers breaks her dad. She stares out through the tears quivering in her eyes like hot mercury and begins the memorized speech, "Dad, I'm sorry. I know...."

He interrupts her. "Hush, child. We've got no time for that. No time for apologies. You'll be late for the party. A banquet's waiting for you at home."[17]

Don't you love that! "Hush, child. We've got no time for that...a banquet's waiting for you at home."

Our teens need to feel that a banquet is awaiting them at home. Our home...their home. They need to know that nothing they can ever say or do would cause us to stop loving them—that we accept them in their "as is" condition.

Of course, it's perfectly fine to confront inappropriate behavior, but even then, the underlying message should be "I will love you no matter what." If their behavior bears consequences, then follow through with them, all the while saying, "I will always love you, but you made a poor decision and the consequences are thus and such. But let me say again how much I love you. Nothing you can do will ever change that fact."

Accept your teen. Accept the fact that he's different from you, and keep in mind that much of what he will or won't say to you depends on whether he feels accepted or rejected.

Bottom Line: If *luxury* were defined as a teen that lives with an accepting parent, could you say that your teen is living in luxury?

BECOMING BILINGUAL

Learning to Speak "Teenager"

Do you know anyone who is bilingual? Although English is her native language, my (Kent) wife Kathy grew up in Peru and speaks Spanish fluently. I am always amazed by the reactions of Spanish-speaking people when she begins speaking to them in their native language. Because many of them are away from their native homelands and here in America, their eyes light up with surprise and delight when she begins speaking to them in their native tongue.

Do you want to see your teen's eyes brighten up like this? Then become bilingual! Learn to speak their native tongue—"teenager"! The next few chapters will give you the linguistic tools for doing just that.

CHAPTER TWENTY-EIGHT

WHY TEENS DON'T RAISE THEIR HANDS ANYMORE

The Communication Rules Have Changed

*My dad's awesome. He knows how to be my parent
and also my friend.*
BRIAN, 13

Do you remember raising your hand in grade school? If you wanted to ask a question or give an answer, you were supposed to raise your hand. Of course, some teachers took this rule to extremes. Want an extreme example? A work associate of mine (Kent) told me that when he would raise his hand in class to ask permission to use the restroom, his teacher made him hold up one or two fingers to indicate exactly what he planned to do. Now that's *extreme!*

To keep from becoming too extreme in parenting our teenagers, some of our communication rules need to be adapted as our children grow older. For example, rules around the house, just like at school, are usually pretty clear for younger children: Always say "Yes, please" or "No, thank you." Don't talk back; no interrupting; listen carefully to instructions. For little kids, the communication rules are pretty clear-cut, similar to the "raise your hand" rule in elementary school.

But house rules change for teenagers. In a manner of speaking, once our children hit adolescence, they're on their way to becoming young adults, and when this happens, the rules need to be "on their way" to adulthood as well. Therefore, we should not speak with them in a childish manner; and in a sense, they should no longer need to "raise their hands" before they are heard.

Please hear what is and is not being said here, though. As little

Johnny grows into a young man, the rules for relating to his parents change. As he matures and his relationship with his parents develops in a healthy way, he will naturally begin to relate to his parents less as a child and more as their equals. Yes, he will always be *their son,* but he won't always be *a child.* And sure, as he grows, continuing to show respect for his parents' position of authority is actually a form of maturity that will prepare him for relating to other authority figures later. However, since Johnny now has reasoning skills and can think abstractly, he *is* forming his own opinions. And guess what…they won't always coincide with his parents'.

So what is a parent to do?

When our own little Johnny was small, we could force our opinion on him and he swallowed everything we said because he had no reasoning skills of his own. He could only think in concrete terms, so he easily assumed that whatever Mom and Dad said had to be true. We could have told him Russia was on Mars, and he would have believed us.

Now he understands the concept of maps and can even read them. In fact, he may have even been to Russia with a youth group while we sat at home wondering what Russia is like. My, how things have changed!

But hold on to your hats—there's more. We used to be bigger than Johnny, so if he said he wouldn't go to his room, we'd just pick him up and put him there. Now, however, little Johnny isn't so little. He is about our size (or perhaps even larger). And he is gaining on us intellectually (or perhaps…you get our point!). To complicate matters even more, we are no longer all-powerful or all-knowing in his eyes. In fact, sometimes he can even solve problems better than we can. And to top it off, he is now even savvy enough to see our character flaws.

So guess what! Talking down to Johnny, forcing our opinions on him, acting like we're all-powerful and all-knowing, physically making him do what we want him to do, or acting like we're beyond reproach are no longer options.

So what *is* a parent to do? How are we to treat this emerging young adult we once called little Johnny?

Actually, our answer may surprise you. But clearly, the only answer is to realize that it is now time to respect little Johnny in a new way. Since he is moving into a new position of being a young adult, our relationship with him must become one of mutual respect.

Although this evolution in the relationship does not change our right to say no to Johnny's request, we now should respect his right to disagree with our viewpoint. In practice, this means that although Johnny may not be allowed to go to Israel with his youth group, we can still respect his opinion and encourage him to share it. If he thinks people are being indirectly controlled by terrorists because they change their travel schedules due to recent terrorist attacks, so be it. Relationally, we might have a rowdy philosophical debate about how his opinion plays out in practical terms, but our authority and caretaker position as a parent may constrain us to respect his opinion while still saying, "No can do right now."

Think about it this way for a moment. Have you ever had a boss you didn't respect? Did you follow his instructions? Probably. Did you enjoy working for him? No. Did you do your best? Perhaps, but it was in spite of him, not because of him. You showed him respect because of his position. But relationally, that was another story.

Now, think of a boss you highly respected. Did you follow his instructions? You bet. Did you enjoy working for him? Definitely. Was it easier to do your very best for the company! Absolutely! Why? Because your respect for the boss wasn't just positional; it was relational.

You are a lot like one of these bosses to Johnny. As a parent, you're still in charge. And by the nature of the teenage "job," Johnny has to follow your instructions. But Johnny will enjoy his "job" much more—and have a greater desire to do his best for the "company"—if his respect for you is as much relational as it is positional. Best of all, he'll be far more apt to interact with you about his life.

The rules have changed all right! And with a little wisdom and sound judgment, you'll see that they've changed for the better.

⨮

Bottom Line: Be the type of "boss" for whom you'd love to work.

CHAPTER TWENTY-NINE

BLASTOFF AND REENTRY

Making Mornings and Evenings Count

*My mom wakes up happy but is usually tired
and irritable by the end of the day. I hope I wake up happy
then stay happy whenever I get married and have kids.*

ELIZABETH, 15

❧

My dear friend Nancy Cobb taught me (Connie) that blastoff and reentry are quick and easy ways to effect change in my marriage. Over time I have discovered how these principles—that are likened to the launching of a spacecraft—also hold true in my relationships with my teenagers.

When a spacecraft is launched, two periods are especially critical— the blastoff and the reentry into the earth's atmosphere. The same is true in the home. Let's take a look:

BLASTOFF

What are mornings like in your home—when everyone is getting ready to "blastoff" to a new day? While it is true that mornings can become especially intense, they're also a perfect time to show your kids you care. And remember, kids who are given lots of tender, loving care have a tendency to talk more than those who have to fend for themselves. The few minutes you spend personally sending your teen off will be one of the best investments you can make in your day—and his!

A few blastoff tips include:

- Go to bed at a reasonable hour so you'll be fresh in the mornings.
- If you have preteen children, make certain they have set bedtimes.

- Spend some time with God and reflect on the day; get up fifteen to thirty minutes earlier than the rest of the household whenever possible.
- Have some juice or cocoa ready for your kids when they come in for breakfast.
- Prepare muffins the night before.
- Wake your kids (and your husband!) up with a smile and a hug. If the gang is out of bed before you are, find them!
- Fix a simple breakfast for them. It doesn't need to be gourmet to be special.
- If you can do only one thing, look them in the eyes and tell them how much you love them. The tone of your voice should be warm and sincere. If this is new, you may feel a bit awkward at first, but keep it up because very soon this part of the daily launch will feel normal.

REENTRY

This is when you and your kids come back together at the end of the day. Your first five minutes with your family at a day's end is often what sets the tone for the rest of the evening.

As your teen's day winds down and he heads for home, what do you suppose he thinks about? Does he envision a place where he's accepted? Can he almost see your warm smile welcoming him home?

If your teen arrives home first, does he eagerly look forward to your arrival? Or does he wonder what kind of mood you'll be in? Does he worry that if you've had a bad day, you'll take it out on him? He shouldn't. He should know without question that he's welcomed in his own home.

When you have guests in your home, undoubtedly you go out of your way to treat them with great courtesy. Certainly you interrupt your own routine to make them feel welcomed.

In a sense, your child is a guest in your home. He's been loaned to you by God to raise, mold, nourish, and love. Your address won't always be his. One day he'll have his own place. His own family. His own traditions. And his own way of welcoming his children back home at the end of the day. Wouldn't it be rewarding to see him "pass on" the way he was welcomed by you!

Here are a few reentry tips:

- Greet your teen warmly—let him know you're happy to be back with him. Even when you don't feel particularly happy, you can still greet him with kindness and welcome him home.
- Study your child: Does he need a few moments to unwind, or does he enjoy instant conversation? A few moments of undivided attention is often all a teenager needs to fill you in on the happenings of the day.
- If you have serious issues you need to discuss with him, don't hit him with them the minute he walks through the door.
- Ask God to help you create a warm, loving atmosphere. Remember, you can't change your teenager, but you *can* change you!

A teen's home should be a special place. It should serve as a "bulwark,"—a place he can approach with eagerness and enthusiasm, knowing he'll find love and acceptance within its walls. It should be a second skin, of sorts. Blastoff and reentry go a long way in providing this kind of environment, which in turn goes a long way in getting your teen to talk.

～≳～

Bottom Line: *Bulwark* isn't an everyday kind of word, but it should be an everyday kind of place for your teen.

CHAPTER THIRTY

THE FUN OF FUN

Laughter Is a Great Medicine

My parents are good at having fun.
They even make doing the dishes fun.
JAKE, 13

⌇

Injecting some fun into your relationship with your teens is a great conversation booster—one of the best, in fact. When it comes to building memories, there's nothing like having fun together. For one thing, laughing and playing together loosen kids up to talk about what's going on in their lives now. Plus, these lifetime memories will be springboards for reminiscing together later.

But many parents make the mistake of expecting their teens' definition of fun to fit into their own. For example, if Dad likes golf, he thinks golfing together on Saturday would be great fun even though Sam keeps hinting that he despises playing golf. Or Mom may be hoping that given enough exposure to antiques, Sarah will get over her opinion that they are nothing but useless pieces of junk. Rather than be discouraged or trying to push their own interests on their children, Dad and Mom would be wise to find out what activities Sam and Sarah enjoy and plan from there.

Having fun with you and relating to you outside your authority figure/wage earner roles will help your teens stay steady in their relationship with you when difficult issues or conflicts arise later. Also, seeing your willingness to invest in them in ways outside of your instructor role will communicate your love for them more broadly.

When you commit to having fun together (and on some days it requires a real commitment because fun doesn't always just "appear"), you invite laughter into the relationship. How long has it been since you and your teen shared a really good belly laugh?

One of the best ways to have fun is to get creative. This creativity will take on different forms for different families, and even different forms for different kids.

Aim to have fun with each of your kids, but also don't forget family fun. Playing darts with my family in the attic bedroom of our old farmhouse is one of my (Connie) favorite childhood memories. The cares of the world and the pressures of growing up seemed to melt away when we did this. I can still hear my parents' laughter when one of us girls would rare back and throw a dart—and hit nothing but the plywood surrounding the board. They taught us that winning was fun, but losing could be too.

Discovering activities that appeal to everyone may take a little effort, but your own attitude will often dictate theirs. Don't be afraid to try something new or make a bit of a fool of yourself. But don't give them the option of bailing out! Instead, tell them you're going out for a family evening together, and then go. ("We will have fun together whether you like it or not!") If your high spirits are met with sulkiness and silence, just ignore their attempts to manipulate you into giving up on the idea of having fun as a family. Once they see the futility of trying to back you down on this, they'll probably give up the struggle, join in, and have fun *accidentally*. Asking for their input on what to do may also help engage them more quickly.

Here's a short list of some ideas to get you started:

- Go to a concert; window-shop at their favorite store; go out for ice cream; rent a hotel in the winter that has an indoor pool; make a video; race go-carts—this is a sure winner; hike; have a Ping-Pong tournament; buy a secondhand telescope and look at the stars; camp; try a new pizza restaurant; play miniature golf or badminton; visit a sports or art museum; watch an old black-and-white movie; drive to a small town and eat at the café on Main Street; go to a drive-in spot and order a cherry limeade; take a drive in the country; build a snowman or make snow ice cream.

For years my (Connie) family and I have set aside time for a family date night each week during the summer. We take turns picking out something fun for the entire family to do. Of course, fun is a matter of opinion, especially when one of the kids chooses to eat at a Japanese restaurant where you have to remove your shoes, and your husband is extremely conscious of how germs are spread. (I think his feet still itch to this day.) We still laugh at the thought of him trying to convince the hostess not to take his shoes.

But we have found that even on those occasions when the event didn't turn out to be that much fun (Shakespeare in the park, for example), the night became special in a completely different way. The memories we made during those times are priceless and have already provided many bridges into great conversation and laughter—we're still talking about many of them today.

Go ahead! Enjoy one another! Break out of your routine and have a little fun. It's inexpensive (depending on the activity you choose, of course), it'll enhance the quality of your lives, and it'll provide a great opportunity to deepen your relationship with your teen.

Seize every opportunity to laugh with your teens. In fact, make it a goal not to just laugh, but to laugh a lot! Parents and teens who laugh together are far more likely to talk together too.

⸎

Bottom Line: *Fun* is not a four-letter word!

CHAPTER THIRTY-ONE

HUGGIE SANDWICHES

Buffering the Negative with the Positive

The only time my parents talk to me is when they want me to do
something, or when they have something negative to say.

DAN, 14

~&~

When my (Connie) girls were little, we used to make "huggie sand-wiches." Wes would get on one side of them while I got on the other, and we'd put our arms around each other and squeeze as tightly as we could. Then we'd all cry out together, "Huggie sandwich." The girls would scream and yell and act like they could barely breathe, but the moment we'd release our arms, they'd ask us to do it again. They loved huggie sandwiches.

Huggie sandwiches are great to use on a teen too—if your arms are strong enough to hold them, that is! This is a fun way to bring a little fun and affection back into the relationship. Your teens may act like you just flew in from the moon, but chances are, they won't mind it much at all.

The "huggie sandwich" strategy can also be played out in other ways too. For example, a corrective statement sandwiched between two positive statements probably won't cause your teen to giggle with glee, but it will

- buffer the criticism from seeming overwhelmingly negative
- let him know that he's still valued, even though there are traits that he needs to improve
- force you to notice and emphasize what he has mastered as well as what he needs to improve

For instance, if you notice that he often forgets to take the trash out on Thursdays, you could say something along the lines of: "I notice how you're always so willing to help me in the yard whenever I ask you to. I really appreciate that! Another thing you could do that would really help is to remember to take the trash out on Thursdays—would you try to do that? Thanks for being willing to learn and change—I really admire that about you."

This is not "schmoozing." This is helping your teen to grow—while leaving his dignity intact. It doesn't take much talent for parents to rant and rave and remind their kids just who's in charge *(and they'd better not forget it)*. However, it does take patience and a healthy, loving perspective to train them up without tearing them down.

Huggie sandwiches also help bear the brunt of a "no" answer. When sandwiching a "no" answer between two positive statements, your teen knows that his request was taken into consideration even though you ultimately assessed that a no was in his best interest. Here, the huggie sandwich softens the disappointment of the "no" answer, while reminding your teen that he is special to you.

For example, you might say something like: "I hear you when you talk about wanting a raise in your allowance. I remember feeling that way when I was a teenager too. However, Dad and I have decided that what we're giving you now is adequate. If you want additional money, we encourage you to find some odd jobs to do. Maybe Mrs. Smith would be interested in hiring you to rake her leaves. Even though we're saying no to your request, we want you to know we think you're a great kid and we love you very much."

Or if you simply can't afford to give him a raise even though you'd love to, the huggie sandwich would look like this: "Dad and I would love to give you a raise in your allowance. We have seen how you wisely stretch your allowance money. But although we recognize that a little extra money would help, we simply can't afford to give you an increase right now. And even though money is tight for all of us now, we want you to know that we recognize what a fine young man you're becoming. So when Dad does get a raise, you'll be the first to know, and we'll revisit this issue then."

With this approach, your teen knows that you have carefully considered and respected his requests, affirmed his feelings, recognized his developing strengths, and expressed your love. The "huggie sandwich" environment is sure to warm up hearts and lead to genuine communication.

~≋~

Bottom line: Huggie sandwiches are the height of fine dining.

CHAPTER THIRTY-TWO

FAMILY MEETINGS
Finding Time to Talk

*How often do my parents and I really connect? Rarely. They're too
busy with their own lives to get involved with mine.*
ELIZABETH, 18

❧

Let's face it—kids and parents are busier today than ever. Between
schoolwork, extracurricular activities, part-time jobs, and hanging out
with friends, our teenagers' lives are filled to the brim. And because
many parents are often too tired to make more than halfhearted efforts
to communicate with their family when they come home at night,
their efforts usually turn out to be superficial at best.

Sure, sometimes those unexpected, wonderful moments just fall
from the sky when we're able to share a special moment with our
teen—maybe it's in the car on the way to a concert or late at night
when you're splitting the last piece of pie while everyone else is asleep.
But generally speaking, our lives are just too fast-paced for these
moments to occur as often as we'd like.

So, what's a parent to do? We suggest weekly family meetings
where you spend time catching up on what's going on in one another's
lives. Certainly we're not saying that this is the only time in the week
for catching up. But we do think that slotting in an hour or two per
week—when everyone is expected to show up and participate—will
help your family stay connected and involved with each other.

Here are some tips for keeping communication flowing smoothly
and well during your family meetings:

- Share with your kids what you want to accomplish in the family
  meeting and welcome their input on how to shape it.
- Find a time that works for everyone. Let them know their

attendance is mandatory. If someone can't make it, change the meeting time for that week.

- Try to make it special in some small way. Maybe go out for dessert at an inexpensive café. Or serve a special (or fun) dinner that night—something as simple as take-out Chinese or grilled-cheese sandwiches will do the trick.

- Use this time to touch base with one another. Ask questions like, "How'd last week go?" or "What's going on next week?"

- Check to see if there's anything your teen is worried about. A casual "Anything bothering you?" or even better, "How can I pray for you this week?" is a nonthreatening way of getting a glimpse of the issues your teen is facing. However, if she doesn't spontaneously share anything, don't press her.

- Keep the atmosphere as light and enjoyable as possible. You want your teens to look forward to these meetings, not dread them. If controversial issues need to be addressed, you may want to discuss them at a different time. The weekly family meeting is meant to be a safe and generally enjoyable time for everyone.

- Set individual and family goals: "How about if we all volunteer two hours per month at the food bank?" or "Maybe you two could rake Mrs. Smith's leaves tomorrow afternoon before she gets home from the hospital?" Start small and work up—otherwise you may become frustrated and give up on this entirely.

- Ask your teens what they want to talk about, *and* listen to what they have to say. Remember, if you begin correcting their thinking the moment they open their mouths, they'll quickly learn not to say anything at all.

- If issues come up that you're unprepared to address right away, commit to a time when you will give them your answer.

- Note positive behavior you've seen in them recently: "That history assignment you turned in was incredible!" "Thanks for going the extra mile by taking Grandma's groceries to her. She felt loved and cared for—thank you!"

- Don't be afraid to share things that are on your mind like "I've got a deadline coming up this week." You don't want to share so openly that kids leave feeling worried or upset. For instance, saying "Pray that my sales will increase this next week" is one thing, but "I don't know where we'll get the money for the house payment if my sales don't increase" is something very different. Be fairly transparent, but not to the point that your teen takes on worries and concerns that are too heavy for her to bear.

- Make certain everyone has time to talk and that your more gregarious kids don't drive the entire meeting. Introspective kids are less demanding of equal attention, but they appreciate it when someone (you!) seeks out their thoughts and opinions.

- End on an upbeat note. Thank them for their investment and involvement in the family. This will esteem them and recognize how their participation contributes to the health of the family unit.

⋙

Bottom Line: Meetings aren't just for the office.

CHAPTER THIRTY-THREE

PEER FEAR

Helping Teens Face Peer Pressure

*Peer pressure can shake your confidence and
is much greater than most adults realize.*
JOANNA, 16

∽

Do you like coming attractions? You know, movie previews? I (Kent)
love them. Since Kathy and I rarely see movies, coming attractions
give us a glimpse of the movie market.

A few years ago, a particular preview caught my eye. It used an
eerie, but effective, catchphrase: *Be Afraid...Be Very Afraid!* I wasn't
enticed to see the movie, but I was afraid!

BE AFRAID...BE VERY AFRAID

What makes you *afraid...very afraid?* Debt? Change? Competition?
These might be just what make your knees knock. But since no two
people are alike, what makes one person anxious is sometimes what
invigorates another.

Teenagers are no different. What frightens one teen is what energizes
another. However, there is one thing that makes every teen's teeth chatter.
The fear of rejection! Rejection makes teenagers *afraid...very afraid.*

FEAR FACTOR

The anxiety of not being accepted is at the root of what experts call
peer pressure. What is peer pressure? It's the stress that is associated with
the desire to "fit in." For teenagers, this stress motivates everything—
dress, speech, behavior—everything! In fact, it's like the television
show *Fear Factor.* Like most game shows, contestants compete for
prizes. But the challenges that the contestants face is what makes *Fear*

Factor different. Each challenge revolves around fear. Jumping from one motorboat to another at speeds of forty miles per hour. Navigating an obstacle course on the ledge of a ten-story building. Swimming in a tank of dead, rotting squids. Eating cow brains. These experiences are designed to see just how far people will go to overcome fear—and win the cash.

Teenagers go to unimaginable lengths to avoid rejection and fit in, often going to the point where they would actually put *Fear Factor* contestants to shame. As Drew, an eighth grader in Omaha once told me, "What I think my friends want controls me. I talk, act, and even dress like them to fit in."

Did you notice what controls Drew? He is controlled by the pressure *he* places on himself—and not necessarily by the pressure put on him by his friends. He thinks his friends want certain things, so his thoughts—whether legit or not—control him.

This is why we call peer pressure *peer fear.* Much of the anxiety teens feel comes from the inward fear of being rejected rather than from outward pressure by peers. The pressure from friends, while at times real, can just as often be imaginary. However, it is important for parents to keep in mind that the inward fear teens feel is always genuine.

TAMING PEER FEAR

How can we get teens to talk to us about peer fear? Try these ideas:

- *Pay attention to timing.* Peer fear is enormous in middle school and the first couple of years of high school. Therefore, be alert early on.
- *Look for signs.* Drew's overwhelming desire to impress friends, sudden changes in speech, dramatic fashion modifications, and moodiness were signs that made me (Kent) think he was struggling with peer fear. While these can be normal features of adolescents, they hit Drew with such intensity that I took notice. If you see similar signs, investigate by asking some caring questions…but be careful not to jump to conclusions.
- *Avoid confusion.* Peer pressure is not necessarily about being cool. It's about fitting in. Although there are always students

who long to be cool, most simply want to belong. So don't confuse the desire to fit in as an unhealthy yearning to be cool. Keep in mind that they aren't necessarily the same.

- *Champion balance.* There's nothing wrong with kids fitting in. However, becoming overly dependent on friends isn't healthy either. Encourage teens to develop a healthy balance between connecting with friends and personal confidence. Even more, model this balance for them.

- *Talk* with, not at. Don't ignore signs of peer fear. Instead, use them as conversational bridges. Ask your teens how it's going with their friends. What do they like and dislike? Get them to describe the greatest pressures they currently face. Communicate how much you care, and steer clear of lecturing. This approach should lead to authentic dialogue.

- *Beware of transitions.* I remember when one teen, Nancy, moved to Omaha. She attended our group, but barely spoke. She wasn't rude, just quiet. Over time it dawned on me that Nancy's quietness had more to do with missing old friends than with her being shy. She's doing great now, but it took her over a year to readjust. Nancy's story is a great example of why it's so difficult for teenagers to move. Since they have invested so much effort into fitting in at school, church, and other places, they feel displaced when they relocate. Take this into consideration when contemplating a move.

  Plus, this fear of transition also explains why many freshmen are excited, yet terrified, of high school. "Who will be my friends?" and "Will I fit in?" are very real questions. Remember this when your teen hits the "freshman-year blues."

- *Separate your teens.* When necessary, separate your teen from friends. Even more, if you sense the need to do this, don't wait and hope things will improve. They won't! Seek wise counsel immediately and take appropriate action.

- *Respect peer fear.* Finally, peer fear is probably the single biggest cause of teenagers' straying away from parents—so develop a healthy appreciation for it. Don't let it paralyze you, but don't blow it off either.

Keep in mind that students who feel accepted, appreciated, and respected by parents are usually not overwhelmed by peer fear.

≈

Bottom Line: Remember, even if pressure from peers is imaginary, the fear is genuine.

NOW WE'RE TALKING!

Moving from Communication to Connection

❧

If you get to the point where your teen is talking to you, you're doing well. But you can still go deeper. You can *connect*. When this happens…*wow!* The following pages will help you do just that.

CHAPTER THIRTY-FOUR

BURY THE COLD TREATMENT
A Conversational Warm-Up

*If I could change one thing about my mom
it would be that she'd stop giving us the "cold treatment" whenever
she gets mad. It makes you feel really, really bad, like you're a loser.*
ANGIE, 14

⁓

Unfortunately, too many teens are growing up in homes where parents fight violently, often leaving a lifelong, negative impact on them. But even in the most ordinary of families, parents disagree from time to time. Recognizing that how parents handle their spousal disagreements vastly impacts their children—and their communication with them—just may tell you that it is time to take a step back and see how you are doing in this area.

How you handle your differences with others, especially conflict with your spouse, is one of the most important lessons you will ever model to your teen.

Some parents assume that it is unhealthy for children of any age to see them disagree with each other. However, this view is far from realistic because, simply put, people don't always see eye to eye on things—especially married people! So when parents take this unrealistic approach, they often resort to the silent treatment when disagreements spring up between them. This way of dealing with conflict is actually more damaging than finding a more straightforward, yet appropriate, way to resolve the conflict. Research shows that children react more negatively to the tension created by parents who give each other the silent treatment than by those parents who discuss their disagreements calmly and rationally. (*Calmly and rationally* being the operative words, of course!)

STOP DOLING OUT THE SILENT TREATMENT

I (Connie) am a reformed "silent treatment" person. During the first few years of my marriage, I was willing to go above and beyond to resolve whatever differences arose between Wes and me. But as the years passed, I decided I was doing too much of the giving. Since I wasn't a person who enjoyed confrontation, I decided I'd dole out the silent treatment instead of looking for creative and effective ways to resolve our differences. And so generously and often, I used silence as a means of avoiding conflict and letting my husband know that I wasn't going to give in. This seemed to work pretty well for me at first glance because I knew I could outwait my husband, and therefore I knew I was going to win. (Does anyone ever really win situations like this?)

No husband—or anyone else for that matter—enjoys this cold treatment. Husbands often have little or no idea why their wives are upset or why they're in the doghouse. They just know things are awfully unpleasant at home, and it seems to have something to do with them.

THE SILENT TREATMENT SHUTS TEENS DOWN

Husbands aren't the only ones who hate the silent treatment—teens are confused by it too. Who enjoys seeing a cold war being lived out right before their eyes, especially in their own homes? No doubt, they have some idea about what's going on and may even understand exactly what sent Mom into her latest frozen state; but over time, they will grow to resent her and her cold ways. Then, as their lack of respect for her increases, they themselves will talk to her less and less. They will begin shutting down for two reasons. First, because their respect for her is dwindling. Second, because they will—either subconsciously or consciously—seek to give her a dose of her own medicine as a means of trying to persuade her from using this tactic.

I (Connie) once asked my girls what one thing they would change about me if they could. They said, "That you would never treat Daddy like *that.*" (The "that" they were referring to was the silent treatment.)

So whether you're a mom or a dad, keep in mind that if you shut down, the rest of your family—including your teenagers—most likely will too. Please learn from my experience of often behaving like a two-year-old rather than like a responsible and loving adult.

PITFALLS TO AVOID WHEN YOU VENTURE INTO VERBAL COMMUNICATION

If you have been using the silent treatment as a means of expressing your anger or making your point, you probably need some tools to help you avoid other pitfalls. As you travel away from the "cold road" with your spouse or teenager—or with anyone else, for that matter—stay committed to adhering to these guidelines:

- Maintain your composure at all times. A person of wisdom realizes the wisdom of holding his tongue.
- Don't resort to name-calling, and don't infer that your spouse or kids are inferior, idiotic, or hopeless.
- Don't swear. Swearing is demeaning and immature…and honors no one. It makes you *look* horrible, while making the rest of the family *feel* horrible.
- Avoid the temptation to slip in a subtle put-down or snide remark. Again, guard your tongue. If necessary, place your hand over your mouth, refusing to engage in the game of one-upmanship…for that is a kind of battle that you don't want to fight or win.
- Ask yourself, "What do my children see me exhibiting most toward them and their dad: Love and respect, or disgust and anger?"
- Instead of making excuses with thought patterns like, "I am who I am," determine to change your ways as needed. Yes, you are who you are, but you may not be the person God wants you to become…and isn't that the person you really want to be?
- Treat others respectfully, even when you feel such treatment is unwarranted. Your children will see your actions and warm up to you. This will grow their respect for you as well.

Cream has a way of rising to the top. When your teens see and experience you treating others well, you will have given them the privilege of seeing cream (you) rise up as an example of communicating maturely, lovingly, and respectfully! And teens tend to talk to people like that.

~~≋~~

Bottom Line: Cold treatment toward others rarely evokes warm communication from your teen.

CHAPTER THIRTY-FIVE

SERVE TOGETHER

Growing Closer

Our family motto is "Do for others what you'd like them to do for you." My parents don't just say it; they really live that way. Thanks, Mom and Dad!

RANDY, 18

⚬⚭⚬

Doing a service project will pull your family together unlike anything else and will open your teen's eyes to those who are less fortunate. Many teens tend to become self-absorbed and think the world revolves around them. Maybe you've made the mistake of allowing this to happen in your home. If so, you can turn that around and help your teen avoid the shock of suddenly leaving home one day and discovering that the world really isn't standing by to meet his every want and need. Doing service projects together will help your child turn some of his attention outward, toward the needs of others. This early wake-up call may also inspire him to be better prepared for the realities of life.

A TEEN'S EYES ARE OPENED TO HUNGER IN OTHERS

A parent of a teen who reached out recalled how surprised she was to see how a simple act of serving others together required so little but reaped so much. Spending an hour serving food reaped the benefit of a total paradigm shift for her son, who had often made fun of people in need. As he stood eye to eye with these people, seeing the hunger in their eyes as well as in their stomachs, he realized that he could be in their shoes. Now, rather than thinking he was better than they were, he became thankful for what he had always taken for granted—a warm bed, a stocked pantry, a family that loved him. "Before, he'd complain if we didn't have the right kind of cookies in the house. Now he thanks me for having any at all," his mother said.

Going to a third-world country isn't necessary. There are plenty of needs to meet right in your own community:

- Serve meals at a homeless shelter.
- Take meals to shut-ins.
- Deliver groceries and run errands for an elderly neighbor.
- Provide a few hours of care for a handicapped child so that his family can have some free time.
- Get to know a young family and offer to baby-sit their youngsters one evening a month so the couple can have a date night.
- Adopt a single-parent family and "fill in gaps" by changing the oil, mowing the lawn, or having them over after church for lunch.
- Adopt a family at Christmas and provide them with food, clothing, and toys.
- Volunteer at a child-care center. The young children will look forward to your visit, and your teens will often adopt exemplary behavior when they realize that the children there see them as role models.
- Visit a nursing home. Just one visit will convince you of the worthiness of this effort. A recent study showed that 85 percent of nursing home residents receive no visitors on a consistent basis.
- Organize a canned-food drive or volunteer to help stock your church's food pantry.
- Adopt a grandparent. Scores of lonely senior citizens have lots of love and timeless wisdom to share.
- Help your teen raise funds to go on a church-sponsored mission trip to a less fortunate country. He will return a different person. When one teen girl we know returned from a mission trip to Mexico with her youth group, she burst into tears when she walked into her home church. Just one week earlier she had been worshiping God in a church building that had no roof and was made of cardboard boxes and chicken wire. The

"pews" were roughly hewn pieces of wood suspended between cement blocks. "The Mexican people are so thankful for what they have," she said, "and they have next to nothing. We have basically everything, but are thankful for so little."

Along with providing the teen with opportunities to develop a servant's heart, serving together often brings opportunities to talk, laugh, and even cry together. Often, this is the kind of communication that you'll both long remember after the actual event has passed. Now that's something worth putting in your scrapbook!

❦

Bottom Line: If you consider serving others to be a high calling, your teen probably will too.

CAN PARENTS BE FRIENDS?
The Issue of Friendship

My parents never worried about being my friends.
They said that one day, if they'd done their jobs right, we'd
most likely end up friends anyway. They were right.

EMILY, 19

❧

"Can I be both a parent and a friend to my teen, or does one of these roles come at the expense of the other?" This is one of the most common questions parents ask us.

PARENTS SHOULD NOT ABANDON THEIR PRIMARY DUTY

Parents often make the mistake of thinking that being friends with their teenagers will make their teens more prone to talk to them. However, we believe that friendship should be the secondary goal. When friendship with their teens becomes their primary goal, parents essentially abandon the primary duty to which they've been called—teaching and training their kids.

When the goal of friendship takes precedence, kids usually end up disrespecting and even disdaining their parents. Kids have an inherent sense of knowing that parents were meant to be leaders first and foremost, not buddies. Unfortunately, the kids are often the ones who do a better job of remembering this than the parents.

When you abandon your parenting role, your child will be the first to notice. Although she may like the freedom and perks that this arrangement initially offers, before long you will command little respect from her. She will quickly discover that she is the one who now sets the tone and wields the power.

Teens don't need to attend a parenting course to know that their parents should be setting limits, saying no, enforcing boundaries, requiring them to pitch in with household chores, and so on. Most likely, they have friends whose parents actually parent, and believe it or not, they wish theirs would step up to the plate and do the same. Internally, they want to see and hear messages that say, "I love you enough to lead you."

PARENTS WHO FORGOT TO BE PARENTS

This parent's experience should serve as a warning to us all on this subject:

> When our son was born, we were so thrilled to be parents that we determined we'd always be his friends, no matter what. In our youthful naïveté, we thought that was the higher calling.
>
> It didn't take long for us to see that our son made demands on us that other children didn't make. When we said no to him, it fell on deaf ears. He would continue his unpleasant behavior until we gave in, which we always did. We found ourselves catering to his every whim, practically standing on our heads to stay on good terms with him. Unbelievably, we still felt we were doing the right thing.
>
> The middle and high school years were bumpy, to say the least. He was placed in detention hall time and again. We attributed this to teachers that didn't understand him. Each time he got into trouble, we bailed him out. We continued assuring him that no matter what, he had lifelong friends in Mom and Dad.
>
> By his late teen years, he refused to go to church, family gatherings, and sometimes even school. He had us wrapped around his finger. Finally, we admitted we were doing something wrong and sought professional help. However, our son blatantly refused to attend any sessions.
>
> What is especially sad in all of this is that our intentions were so good. We wanted a close relationship with him, and we thought friendship was the way to attain that. In our efforts to be his friends, we forgot to be his parents. This has resulted

in his having no respect and little love for us.

Parents, don't ever think that friendship is the highest form of love. Parenting—setting rules, following through, being consistent in discipline, and yes, loving them enough to be tough— is a far higher calling. We suspect, though we'll never know, that when done well, this will result in what we so wanted all along—a deep and lasting friendship with one's child.

BE A LEADER FIRST, AND A FRIEND SECOND

We encourage you to not default on what God has called you to do. Laying down your responsibilities as a parent is not a shortcut to getting your teen to talk to you. In actuality, sacrificing your role as leader in exchange for the role of being your child's friend will actually short-circuit your communication with her.

Another common misnomer is that parents enhance their teens' self-esteem when they give in to them on every issue. This is a dangerous practice. Healthy self-esteem is derived when a child is loved enough to be taught right from wrong and to respect those in authority over her; giving in doesn't do this.

Soon your teen will be on her own and living out from under your roof. This is the time when your parenting grip will loosen while your friendship grip is strengthened. Ideally she will still ask for your input and wisdom, and ideally you will wait for her to ask for your input before you jump in with your opinions. When this time comes and she takes full responsibility for charting her own course, don't you want to be able to look back over the breadth of your parenting life and say, "By the grace of God, we did it!"?

What joy it will be to watch your child spread her wings and fly. But if the parenting role has been forsaken too early in lieu of friendship, she'll be spreading clipped wings and may never fly as high as she could have otherwise.

If you keep first things first, your child will one day thank you!

⤳

Bottom Line: Specialize in soaring, not wing clipping!

CHAPTER THIRTY-SEVEN

DISCOVER THEIR PASSIONS
What Makes Their Hearts Beat Faster?

If you want your kids to talk to you, do things they enjoy doing instead of making them conform to your idea of fun.
TIM, 15

~

Recently my (Connie) husband and I took a young couple out to eat. As we chatted about many topics, I noticed how Bob kept coming back to the subject of my writing. What had prompted me to write in the first place? How did I find a publisher? How long did I write each day?

Finally, it hit me: Bob must be a writer at heart. "Bob," I asked, "do you like to write?"

"I love to write," he said. "It's my passion."

As we talked about writing for the rest of the evening, we saw an energy and fire in Bob that we hadn't seen before. It was as though he came alive and shared his heart with us in new ways.

Tapping into teens' passions will also get them talking. You will visit places that few others are privileged to explore when you discover and continue to probe for what they are most passionate about.

WHAT ENERGIZES YOUR TEEN?

Your teen's passion may or may not mirror your own—more than likely it won't. But don't let that difference stop you from learning all you can about what energizes your teen.

Keep in mind that passions are different than interests. Your teen may enjoy basketball, but this doesn't qualify it as a passion. We *like* to do lots of things, but we *love* to do very few. Those things we love to do are what we categorize as passions.

SHARE IN THEIR PASSIONS

We know one teen whose passion is singing. To share in her passion, her parents have learned all they can about music. To support her, they gave her an hour of recording time in a studio for a Christmas gift. The recording is yet to be made, but just knowing her parents have supported her in this tangible way has caused her to chat nonstop about her hopes and dreams for the future.

Another teen we know has a passion for baseball. Lots of kids are interested in baseball, but for this young man, it is truly his passion. He hopes to one day make it to the big leagues. Do you think his parents are telling him that his chances of actually making it big are about one in ten billion? Absolutely not! Instead, they've become baseball fanatics themselves. They stay current on who's winning, who's losing, and which players are having dynamite seasons. They're into what their son is into because they want to share this special part of his life with him. This has created a lot of great memories as well as many late-night conversations. Someday his dream may go up in smoke. Then what? "If he never makes it big, he'll always love the game, and we'll always enjoy sharing his love of the game with him," his parents told us.

Do you know what your teen loves to do? Maybe he hasn't discovered it yet. If so, help him discover this. If you offer him lots of opportunities and then watch for which ones he gravitates back to, you'll discover what makes his heart beat a little faster.

DON'T FORCE YOUR PASSION UPON YOUR CHILD

A word of warning though: Don't try to force your own passion upon your child by trying to convince him that your passion is his. Passions can't be forced. They come naturally and are discovered or developed over time. Maybe you think your daughter has what it takes to become a concert pianist, and maybe she does, but insisting that playing piano should be her passion will only breed frustration and resentment in her. Sure, encourage her to do well and to play with excellence, but don't force it upon her. The same is true for sports or writing or any other special interest!

WAYS TO HELP YOUR TEEN EXPLORE HIS PASSION

Exploring a passion doesn't have to cost a lot of money. If your teen's passion is rockets, you don't have to fly to Florida for the next launch. Together you can do things as simple as discussing newspaper articles and news programs that cover the launch, building a model, visiting an aeronautical museum, and even renting movies with plots that involve rockets.

We know of one family whose daughter loved to play basketball. And since neither parent could teach her a jump shot, they hired a gifted student athlete to work with her twice a week. Before long, a jump shot—and an especially thankful daughter—emerged.

In our experience, we have found that kids' exuberance spills over into hearty, fun-filled conversations with their parents. This kind of sharing is often a wonderful bridge to discussing even deeper issues.

Bottom Line: A teen's passions and his vocal cords are closely linked.

CHAPTER THIRTY-EIGHT

OPEN HOUSE

Making Your Home Teen-Friendly

*Come over any Friday...there's always something happening
at my house on the weekends!*

ERIN, 16

~≈~

Teenagers live for the weekend and their favorite pastime during this
two-day break is just hangin' out. Talking, laughing, connecting with
friends...this is the stuff that makes weekends memorable for them.
Amazingly, they don't need tons to do, just a place to kick back and
enjoy.

So here's our question: Is your house this kind of a place?

If you really want to get your teen talking to you, you need her to
be around you. And one great way to have her around, especially on
the weekends, is to transform your home into a student hangout.

THE RETRO HOUSE

Mark and Libby have done just that. Their basement is a teen-friendly
spot where their son's friends gather each weekend night. Setting the
stage for a great place for teens to be teens is a '50s diner motif, modern amenities like a Sony PlayStation and a DVD player with sur-
round sound, tons of food and sodas, music, comfortable sofas, and
two parents that don't freak out over spills and stains.

Obviously, Mark and Libby have invested lots of resources to create
this environment. However, realizing that many homes open to students on weekends are more like frat houses than safe houses, they
have created a fun place that is also safe. Unlike other places where
alcohol and other unmentionable activities flow because parents take
the posture that "Kids are going to get wild, and we'd rather have them

go crazy here than out on the streets," Mark and Libby take a much different approach. Their philosophy is: "We encourage Max to invite his friends over, and we enhance the offer by making our house as teen-friendly as possible. However, we are always home when his friends are around. It's not that we don't trust him; we simply don't want to place him in pressure situations, especially in our own home. So we make sure we're home, but assume more of a supervision posture rather than a surveillance stance. It's a 'protection by being around' approach that works well."

Obviously, the cool atmosphere Mark and Libby have created attracts teens; but their tactic of being around—without being overbearing—keeps teens coming back. This modus operandi has created a safe, teen-friendly place for students to blow off the school-week blues, but be in a safe place too.

THE GUIDANCE-COUNSELING HOUSE

Dave and Diane don't have the resources that Mark and Libby do. But even though their home is quite small, their house attracts just as many teenagers. Every weekend, teenagers sit in their living room…eating pizza or munching on chips, listening to music, playing games, or watching videos. Even more amazing, Dave and Diane are often in the middle of all the activity and both of their teens love it. As their son, Brian, says, "Our mom and dad are pretty cool, and my friends like having them around. But they also know when to give us space."

Their daughter Jessica chimes in, "Yeah, and when they don't, all we have to do is tell them, and they back off. They really listen, and I respect that."

THESE PARENTS KNOW NOT TO ACT
LIKE ADOLESCENTS

Even though Dave and Diane are more visible to the kids than Mark and Libby are, they aren't overbearing. They also don't try to fit into the teenager scene (parents acting like adolescents is a huge turnoff to teens), but they have learned how to relationally connect as caring adults. Many nights start out with everyone playing games and scarfing down food, yet end up with Dave or Diane sitting around the kitchen table listening to students talk about real-life issues. Most of these teens view Dave and Diane as older, trusted friends whom they can go to for advice.

BONUS BENEFITS

Both couples have created very different environments, yet each setting is teen-friendly. Additionally, both believe making their homes teen hangouts has two extra benefits. First, creating a teen-friendly environment leads to special conversations with their own kids. Once all the friends go home, these couples and their teenagers often get into late-night chats. You know, the ones that start when you're stretched out across the couch or cleaning the kitchen together. It starts off with small talk, and then turns into a time of deep discussion. Each conversation is special and builds authentic trust between you and your teen. According to these couples, this is a huge dividend to having an open-house policy!

Second, an open home allows parents to catch a glimpse of teenage culture. Parents get to know their teens' friends by actually seeing what they do and hearing what they say. They also see how their own teens interact with their friends. These benefits give these parents a better understanding of the world in which their teens live and how their kids are doing in that world. They see firsthand some of the influences and pressures their teenagers face. An open-house strategy allows parents to put their fingers on the pulse of their teenagers' world. Knowing about this world—that they would not have otherwise even known existed—enables them to help their kids navigate through these turbulent waters.

Is your house teen-friendly? It might take some work to create the right, safe environment for your teens and their friends. But the conversations, memories, and insight will be well worth the effort!

~~

Bottom Line: Transform your living quarters into an open house!

DO YOU PROMISE
NOT TO TELL?

The Importance of Confidentiality

I don't trust my mom.
Whenever I tell her something, it comes back to haunt me.
AARON, 21

❦

It's difficult to count the times teenagers have said to me (Kent), "I need to tell you something, but you have to promise not to tell anyone, *especially my parents.*" Early on, I was quick to make this promise. However, my attitude changed when students shared thoughts about suicide, drug use, or other harmful behaviors. I bagged any thoughts of being a hero and developed this standard response: "I promise to listen carefully and do what I believe is the very best thing for you."

Most students trusted me enough to talk, and over the years I've heard dreadful stories about pregnancy, drugs, suicidal thoughts, and occult involvement. However, by and large I've heard about normal teenage stuff. When I have asked teens why they don't want to talk to their parents, they have invariably said, "Are you crazy? I couldn't tell my parents; they'd never understand."

If I tried to persuade them otherwise, they often came back with, "Yeah, but I can't trust my parents. If I tell them, the whole world will know." This response always stumped me. How could I recommend they tell their parents if their parents weren't trustworthy?

BE TRUSTWORTHY

Confidentiality is huge for teenagers. They simply won't talk to us if they can't trust us. So how can we gain their trust? *First, we must be a safe place where they can share their confidences without fear that we will tell others what they have told us.*

We've met hundreds of parents who humiliate their teens with their blabbing. Some do it to get laughs, while others just don't think about the end result. But regardless of the reason, teens make the assessment that their parents can't keep a secret.

A twenty-one-year-old recently told me, "I don't trust my mom. Whenever I tell her something, it always comes back to haunt me." In high school, he accidentally let it slip who he liked. He made his mom promise not to say anything to anybody. Yet three days later at church, his best friend's mother started asking questions about the "crush" he had on a girl. "Kent, I didn't know what to say. I stood there in disbelief."

Another young man recently told us, "I can tell my parents anything." And he does just that; he goes to them for all kinds of advice— dating, friendship, school. He seeks their counsel for various reasons, but at the top of his list is trust. He trusts their opinion; but most of all, he trusts them.

Authentically Apologize When Necessary

The second way to prove our trustworthiness is by sincerely apologizing when we let information slip out. When we accidentally forget to keep a secret, making excuses is the worst thing we can do. Instead of disregarding how important confidentiality is to our teen, it's far better to humbly ask for his forgiveness. If we authentically apologize, he will begin to trust us again.

Seeking Counsel

Finally, here are two guidelines for seeking legitimate counsel when our teens tell us something in confidence:

First, never promise that you won't tell your spouse about the matter. For instance, if your son says, "Mom, I need to tell you something, but you can't tell Dad," don't make this promise.

Instead, say something like, "Honey, I can't make that promise. You know your dad and I work through all important decisions together." Promise to listen carefully to all he says, but help him respect your marriage partnership by telling him that you will talk to your husband about the situation if you think it is something he needs to know.

Even if you are divorced or your spouse cannot keep secrets, it is important for you to tell your teen that you will do what you think is right. Then, if there is a reason why you need to tell your spouse, you can do so in good conscience.

Second, seeking outside help may sometimes be needed, particularly in cases like your son telling you a friend is contemplating suicide or your daughter telling you someone was raped. To avoid having to break a confidence, begin the conversation with something like: "Son, you obviously need to get something off your chest. I want you to feel safe with me. I will listen carefully to everything you tell me. But I want you to know that I will get extra counsel if I think I need to talk to someone else about this. I love you and want what's best for you. Trust me."

Then, after all is said and heard, keep the promise you just made.

❦

Bottom Line: Confidentiality is far more than just keeping secrets; it's also about being trustworthy.

A LITTLE SEX TALK

Talking with Your Teen about the Guy/Girl Thing

❧

What's one of the top issues that must be addressed—early and often—during the teenage years? The guy/girl thing! Dating, sexuality, love, romance…. When the onslaught of our oversexed culture is coupled with a teenager's natural curiosity about these issues, the guy/girl thing is on teenagers' minds 24/7. Wise parents do not delay helping their teens shape their values about this topic.

The next few chapters are packed full of ideas on how to talk *with* your teen about sexuality, dating, and purity. Even more, they'll also help you figure out ways for helping your teen feel comfortable talking with you about these very important subjects.

CHAPTER FORTY

ANATOMY 101

Beating the System to Talking about the Body and Sex

My dad's talk was too little…and much too late.
DOUG, 14

⁓

Many people today are fascinated with sex. You can't watch TV or pick up a magazine without the topic coming up…several times. For instance, a recent study indicated:

> Four out of five situation comedies on TV have sexual content, and a third of the characters engaged in sexual intercourse on TV are twenty-four or younger—that includes high schoolers Pacey and Joey on the teenage favorite *Dawson's Creek*. And according to a report from the Kaiser Family Foundation, movies are even more sexually saturated—nine out of ten include sexual content. The Kaiser study found that a third of all teenagers say the media encourages them to have sex.[18]

Obviously, sex dominates pop culture.

But it also dominates the education system. SIECUS (Sexuality Information and Education Council of the United States) is a nonprofit organization that "develops, collects, and disseminates information, promotes comprehensive education about sexuality, and advocates the right of individuals to make responsible sexual choices."[19]

Their Web site leads one to believe that they think schools should play a major, if not *the* major, role in providing both factual information and moral guidelines for sexual choices. They even promote the idea that sex education should start as early as kindergarten and have published *Guidelines for Comprehensive Sexuality*

Education: Kindergarten–12th Grade.[20]

While we recognize that many parents are very concerned about what's taught through pop culture and the education system, we will address a different concern in this chapter. Namely, who is teaching your kids about their bodies (both the factual stuff and moral stuff)? Is it you? Or have you passed the buck to pop culture and the school system? Who is teaching your teens the truth about the one topic that probably interests them most?

With or without your input, your teens are going to learn about their bodies. What's more, they're going to learn about them much earlier than you did. Formal sex education in today's world starts in early grade school. But you're kidding yourself if you think that's the only place where kids pick up information and values. There are an abundance of other avenues as well. We've already mentioned TV and movies, but what about friends, magazines, and the Internet? Even churches are actively addressing the issue. Therefore, good parenting means proactively tackling this issue head-on…early and often.

Unfortunately, parents often seem to be the only ones postponing their own dissemination of information about this subject to their kids. What's more, by the time many parents get around to it, Joe or Julie have already heard it all (either accurately or inaccurately, and usually not including the moral values the parents hold).

One teen said it this way: "My parents don't know how much sex happens around me in my daily environment. It's commonplace. And my dad's talk was too little…and much too late." Amazingly, this teen is in ninth grade. That's right, ninth grade! And this is just one example out of dozens (if not hundreds) we've heard from students, some as young as sixth and seventh graders.

Parents *must* be a teen's primary sex educators. If we aren't, how will our values be passed on? When our teen ends up getting involved in questionable behavior, how can we question his action if all we've done is passively hand him a book or had "the talk" with him? Do such simplistic actions adequately equip him to face the pressures associated with the modern view of sexuality? Moms and Dads, this discussion is not a one-time event. It's ongoing. Therefore, we must:

- be direct
- be blunt
- share our wisdom and insights (paying attention to timing, of course)
- ask and answer questions
- not be embarrassed
- be honest
- be available (and make sure our teen knows we are available)
- let him know he can come to us and talk about anything
- let him know there are no dumb questions or statements

Most of all, *we must be intentional.* The more open we are, the more likely our teens will be to talk with us openly. Remember, they're curiously and anxiously looking for a safe place to ask tough questions. Let's be that safe place!

If you're struggling with the idea of what to say or how to say it, the next few chapters should help. Plus, there are some great resources listed in the Appendix. The key, however, is action. Don't be passive on this one.

⌐≈⌐

Bottom Line: Be the one to talk to your teen about intimate issues.

CHAPTER FORTY-ONE

AND THEY CALL IT...
PUPPY LOVE

Teenage Love and Romance

I'm madly in love!
BETHANY, 13

❧

"He's tall and blond with blue eyes. He's incredibly tan and has a gorgeous smile. And he's so nice. In fact, yesterday he said hi to me in the hall. I think he's the one!"

I (Kent) can't begin to count how many chats like this I've had with teenage girls. Yet the conversations I've had with guys are even more humorous. "Kent, I mean…she's awesome. She's…she looks like…she makes me feel like…man, I can't describe her. But trust me, dude, she's awesome."

Okay, okay, so teenagers (especially younger teens) develop crushes. And yeah, they get overly emotional and pretty irrational. But in spite of all this, there is one mistake parents must avoid like the plague when it comes to teenage romance: *Don't belittle your teen's feelings.*

Parents pay a huge price when they tease thirteen- or fourteen-year-olds about their starry-eyed feelings for someone of the opposite sex. Sure, it's puppy love. But isn't puppy love real to a puppy?

The truth is, the romantic feelings that adolescents and young teenagers experience, especially when they have recently entered puberty, are first-time feelings. They're raw and passionate, probably the "realest" feelings they've ever felt. To them, their feelings of love are the real deal. When you throw cold water on your teen by treating him as though his feelings are silly, you demean him. The end result? He will quickly find someone else to talk to about this tender topic...someone he can trust not to chuckle when he talks about his feelings. You see, when you negate his feelings, you've instantly come off as being insensitive, uncaring, out of touch, irreverent, and cruel— all because of a few careless comments.

Parents, here's a news flash for you: Teenage love is enormously serious to teenagers, even the silly, first-time romantic feelings experienced by middle schoolers. Therefore, be tactful and sensitive about their feelings. Don't use phrases like "smoochy-smooch" or "someone has a girlfriend." Teens hate this kind of parental babble. You may think it's cute, but trust us, your teen doesn't.

Instead, when your teen tells you that he is in love, seize this opportunity to strengthen your relationship with him. How you respond to your teen's first romantic feelings will set the table for the conversations you will have (or not have) with him throughout the remainder of his teenage years. If you are sensitive, caring, respectful, and attentive, you'll score huge points in the "approachable" category. You might even have an outside shot at becoming a trusted advisor!

What's more, you can help your teen process his or her feelings. What an awesome opportunity to gradually teach your son or daughter that there is much more to love than feelings. And since more is caught than taught, walking through your teen's experience with him will teach him loads more about love than a stand-alone lecture ever could.

So when your "puppy" falls in love, don't laugh. Instead, keep in mind that this could indeed be one of the most teachable moments you will ever have with your teen...and definitely an experience to build upon.

⌒≈⌒

Bottom Line: When it comes to puppy love—actually, when it comes to anything at all—build up instead of belittle.

CHAPTER FORTY-TWO

GOOD SEX

Is There Such a Thing?

Oral sex is all too common at my school.
SARAH, 16

❧

Okay, we know, there's no way to adequately deal with this topic in just one chapter, especially now that our oversexed culture has created a glut of dilemmas for teenagers. Yet with all the negatives so prevalently surrounding the subject of sex in our culture today, we must be careful not to communicate that sex is bad or disgusting. In the right context, sex is good…even *great!* Here are a few ideas for helping your teens understand and embrace this truth:

CLARITY

At a 2002 conference for school superintendents, a speaker reported that the number-one problem administrators of middle schools face with students today is oral sex. Our instant response to such reports is, "What's the world coming to?" But let's not forget to ask another question: "What can we do about it?"

The best thing parents can do to help their teens deal with society's confusing messages about sex is to clearly define what sex encompasses. For example, is it just intercourse, or does it include foreplay and oral stimulation?

Next, communicate the appropriate context for sex. Is sex only for marriage, or is it okay when people really "love" each other?

Finally, parents need to be able to back up their beliefs. Are their values just opinions or does Someone higher define the absolute truth about this?

Wondering what standards you should teach? Check out
1 Thessalonians 4:3–8 for what God says about sexual standards.

Knowing what you believe, why you believe it, and being able to articulate those beliefs with boldness and clarity is crucial. If you don't lead your teen in developing standards, who will? Perhaps you don't hold to firm standards about this yourself. Maybe you are still deciding your position on these issues. If so, please know this: Your waffling on this issue, you're basically saying "anything goes" to your kids. So find someone you trust and respect that holds to biblical principles and ask him (or her) to help you determine how you will help your teen navigate through these very choppy waters.

TIMING

Since high school students usually live out the values they have developed in middle school, age thirteen is too late to start helping them clarify standards. The time to start talking seriously about sex is when kids reach the fourth or fifth grade.

REMINDERS

After the "birds and the bees" talk, many parents think, *Whew, I'm glad* the talk *is over. I've done my job.*

Wrong!

Sex education doesn't stop with *the talk;* it's an ongoing dialogue. Teenagers need constant reminders about what beliefs to hold on to and why. They also need to be regularly assured that no question is dumb or off-limits.

This ongoing approach is crucial. Kenneth, a middle-aged guy we know explained it this way: "My parents did most things right. However, my one complaint is that they didn't regularly discuss sexual standards with me. I knew what they believed, but I needed to hear them say it more. I needed to be reminded of why these standards were so important."

RELATIONSHIP

At the top of our list of reasons why teens engage in sex before marriage is: a breakdown in the parent/teen relationship. Sexually active students we've talked with commonly say that their parents are just too busy and relationally disconnected to care.

Yet as Josh McDowell says, "As parents provide the proper emotional, spiritual, and psychological stability for their child in a loving relationship, closeness increases and temptation to seek intimacy through sexual involvement decreases…. If you want to insulate your child from many sexual pressures, develop a close open relationship of mutual respect and love."[21]

HELPING TO ENSURE THAT THERE ARE NO REGRETS

When talking about sexuality with teens, don't overlook talking about the consequences associated with mistakes. The obvious costs can be unwanted pregnancies and sexually transmitted diseases, but the emotional costs can be just as expensive. For instance, when a girl gives herself to a guy, she gives more than her body; she also gives her heart. And once she lets go of her heart, she never gets it back in the same shape. The more encounters she has before marriage, the more damaged her heart becomes. Even if she wants to give her heart to her husband someday, she may only have a few pieces left.

The emotional cost for boys is different, but still expensive. They have photographic memories. One friend told us: "My parents promoted what the Bible teaches about sex: that it's only beautiful within the context of marriage. They taught going lower than the "turtleneck" level is off-limits until marriage. I bought into their view for most of my teenage years. However, during a really rebellious period when I walked away from the faith, I remained a virgin, but broke the "turtleneck" rule. Even when I started following God again, I still stumbled several times. Although I'm glad I remained a virgin before marriage, I wish I would have waited in other areas too. There are permanent memories, like freeze-framed photos in my head, and I fight an ongoing battle to honor my wife by not walking down memory lane."

Have you met people with similar regrets? We have! However, we have yet to find a person who remained pure before marriage say, "I regret not messing around beforehand. What a mistake."

Has your teen already slipped? Maybe he'd like to start over, but feels like his mistake has tarnished him for life. Discuss "second virginity" with him. This is the idea of starting fresh and living pure from this point forward.

FOCUS ON PURITY, NOT JUST ON WAITING TO HAVE SEX

Perhaps the biggest mistake parents make in talking about sex is zeroing in on abstinence only. A far better approach is to focus on *purity*. Do you see the difference? If we focus on abstinence alone, our teens only hear, "Wait until you're married to have sex." This leaves all other variables open for interpretation. However, focusing on purity puts a completely different skew on the variables and usually makes teens contemplate more deeply and assess more narrowly what they will and won't do.

A HUNK OF SOD

Finally, here's an illustration that answers the question that teenagers most commonly ask: If two people really care for each other, why is it wrong to make love? When answering this question, consider this analogy:

If your parents want a well-groomed yard with as few weeds as possible, they have to work hard. But after a long day's work, when they look out on the lawn, you hear them comment, "Doesn't the yard look beautiful?" And it does, because the sod is cared for and in its proper place.

But if you dig up a hunk of that sod with a shovel, take it in the house and put it on your mom's rug, what will she say? "Get that dirt out of here!" Why would she say that? Just a few minutes ago she said it was beautiful. Is it beautiful sod or nasty dirt? That depends on what you do with it. In the yard, it's beautiful. On the rug, it's dirt.

That's similar to the way you [teens] should handle your sexuality. If you use it in marriage...then it's beautiful. If you use it outside of marriage...then it becomes dirty.[22]

❧

Bottom Line: Be proactive! Talk with your teen—early and often—about *purity.*

CHAPTER FORTY-THREE

FOR GUYS ONLY

The Big M

We have to do it; it's part of our nature.
JERRY SEINFELD

❧

"Are you the master of your domain?"

Seinfeld fans know exactly what this means. It revolved around a contest in which Kramer, George, Elaine, and Jerry bet to see who could hold out the longest. Hold out from what? They never said it, but clearly they were talking about "The Big *M.*" Still don't know? It's withstanding the temptation to masturbate.

If you saw the episode, you know how realistic the depiction was. The writers took an unmentionable activity and projected the message that "everyone does it." And by comparing it to shaving, they said "men have to do it" because it's "part of their nature."

Is masturbation really that big of a deal? *Yes!*

"Statistics vary, but all agree that more than 60 percent of females and more than 90 percent of males have been involved in masturbation at some time in their lives."[23] What's more, while many female adolescents experiment with masturbation, most male adolescents regularly practice it. I (Kent) even remember a joke in college: "Ninety-five percent of guys masturbate, the others lie about it."

Like we said, it's a big deal.

BE CONCERNED, BUT DON'T PANIC

When hearing these facts, many parents (especially moms) initially panic. "Oh no, my sweet boy is becoming a sex-crazed pervert. What do I do?"

First of all, don't let false assumptions lead you down the road to panic. Masturbation is not a weird problem practiced only by sex-crazed perverts. As stated above, most people, especially males, experiment with masturbation. However, because teens can wind up practicing compulsive masturbation or using pornography to enhance the experience, you do need to show concern. Plus, if a person becomes addicted, it can be an issue later on. One man explains the dangers from his own personal experience:

> Once married, I was sure stopping would be easy. During the first months of marriage, I didn't even think of masturbating. My wife and I were caught up in the excitement of exploring one of God's most pleasurable gifts. Yet within six months, I started again. It had nothing to do with a lack of sexual fulfillment…it wasn't about a loss of love…it had to do with the pace of life. I did everything at one speed—fast. Since I was constantly busy, masturbation was quick and easy.[24]

Obviously, if masturbation can someday be a substitution for intimacy between a husband and wife, we need to help ensure that our teenage sons don't become addicted.

WHAT DO I DO?

"Okay, you've told me that I should be concerned, but you still haven't answered the question: *What do I do?*"

Talk.

"Talk?"

That's right, talk.

Since there is a high probability that your son will experiment with masturbation, it's best to learn to talk about it with him. As you consider this, keep in mind that television programming talks about it, teachers and youth workers talk about it, and even teenage guys talk about it among themselves. So, if you want him to have your input on how his values are shaped, get talking and keep talking.

Are you willing to show your son that helping him shape his values is so important that you will maturely discuss difficult issues with him? If not, what message does he receive if his parents choose to keep their heads in the sand?

WHAT DO I SAY?

Hopefully at this point you are saying to yourself, "Okay, I'll bring it up. But what do I say?"

Consider the approach suggested by James Dobson.

> I would suggest that parents talk to their twelve- or thirteen-year-old boys in the same general way my mother and father discussed this subject with me. We were riding in the car, and my dad said, "Jim, when I was a boy, I worried so much about masturbation. It really became a scary thing for me because I thought God was condemning me for what I couldn't help. So I'm telling you now that I hope you don't feel the need to engage in this act when you reach the teen years, but if you do, you shouldn't be too concerned about it."[25]

What compassion! Is it time for you to have this conversation with your son?

WHEN AND HOW OFTEN DO I BRING THIS SUBJECT UP?

You may be wondering, *But when is the right time to talk about this?* Great question! After all, it doesn't exactly fall into the same category as the weather!

Be sure to say something when your son begins to experience physical changes like growth spurts, a deepening voice, muscular development, and hair growth. But that's not the only time. We believe the subject needs to be addressed more than once. For instance, talking about addictive behaviors, pornography, and even the danger of continuing to masturbate after marriage are good topics to discuss as teens get older.

WHO SAYS WHAT?

Finally, if there is a father in the house, this is definitely his area. It's not that Mom has nothing to say, but this topic best fits into a man-to-man discussion. Because these conversations will be awkward for your son, having this discussion with someone who wrestles with it as "part of his nature" will make talking about this a little easier. If there is no father, find a trusted uncle, pastor, or friend and ask him if he will discuss this subject with your son. I (Kent) have done this for a number of single moms.

Remember, each time you talk about something difficult like this, you crack the door open for significant conversation and lay the groundwork for amazing candor between your teen and you.

◆

Bottom Line: If you have a boy, "The Big *M*" is an issue…so talk.

CHAPTER FORTY-FOUR

FOR GIRLS ONLY

Questions, Questions, Questions

There's this boy who pulls my bra strap and I hate it.
What should I do?[26]

TIRED OF BEING POPPED, BALTIMORE, MARYLAND

~

While some girls are more private than others, most girls love to gather as much information as possible about the topic of sexuality. So if you have girls, be ready for some lengthy conversations whenever you bring this subject to the discussion table.

QUESTIONS, QUESTIONS, QUESTIONS

I (Connie) found this out firsthand when I volunteered at church to facilitate a series called "Preparing for Adolescence." This was one curious group of sixth-grade girls! Their questions included: *Is the vagina where a girl urinates? How does a man's penis get inside the woman (a few didn't realize this took place)? What are wet dreams, and are they bad? What is masturbation—how does a guy do it; how does a girl do it; is it normal; do people go to hell if they masturbate? Is homosexuality wrong— how does this occur in men and women? Is there just one sperm and one egg?* And perhaps the most common one, *Does sex feel good?*

Remember, these were sixth-grade girls. Not eighth, not tenth. Sixth!

TEACH HER TO DEMAND RESPECT

When it comes to talking about sexuality with girls, there are many particulars to cover, yet one essential should be addressed early and often: *How should girls expect guys to treat them?*

The answer is easy—with respect.

Yet in reality, many guys don't show girls (or later, women) respect. If the truth be told, many of them see girls as objects to be conquered instead of people to honor and respect.

Shouldn't girls just ignore these guys? Of course. But this is actually trickier than it appears because teenage guys can be brilliant con artists.

You see, girls want relationship. They long for intimacy and connectedness. Teenage guys, on the other hand, have more physical impulses. They crave visual and sensual stimulation. Any guy who doesn't learn to control these impulses is dangerous. However, guys who con their prey by hiding their true motives behind a facade of appearing to be honorable are even more dangerous. These sweet-talkers use their knowledge of what girls want (relationship and love) to get want they want (foreplay and sex). To make matters worse, a girl who yearns deeply for relational intimacy may end up giving in to one of these con artists. And one tragic reality usually holds true: Once a girl "puts out," the possibility of gaining intimacy with her former suitor quickly disappears.

THE #1 MESSAGE: DON'T PUT OUT

In light of this, the number-one message teenage girls need to hear from parents is, "Don't put out! Letting a guy get physical with you *never* leads to relational depth. It's a treacherous shortcut that runs into an ugly dead-end."

Only gentlemen that consistently show respect for her inner person *and* her body should be allowed on her radar screen as candidates for relationship.

She must also be warned that even good guys struggle to keep their hands to themselves. Even if she meets a young man who legitimately likes her and treats her honorably, she must continue to be vigilant. If she allows him to cross the line and touch her inappropriately, his natural male tendencies will kick in, and he will see her as an object to conquer. Guys need to do their part and keep their hands to themselves, but girls need to just as strongly ensure that inappropriate touching, petting, and foreplay are off-limits.

DRESS APPROPRIATELY AND MODESTLY

Girls can hinder implementation of this "hands off" policy by dressing inappropriately. Because guys are visually stimulated, what appears fashionable to girls is often way too revealing for guys. If girls are serious about wanting guys' respect, they must learn to keep their high-fashion clothes modest.

Amazingly, moms are sometimes the greatest stumbling block to modesty. When I've (Kent) shared these thoughts with moms, some blow me off and say, "You've got to be kidding. My daughter's clothes are cute, not sensual." These moms just don't seem to understand how easily males are stimulated.

If you're the mother of a teenage daughter, please hear this: Guys are intensely driven by what they see. If girls wear something even remotely revealing, she is in danger of being seen as an object. Sure, guys need to learn control, but young ladies should help by dressing modestly. It's a two-way street.

You'd be shocked at what guys think is revealing—spaghetti strings, tank tops, rib huggers, and sports bras. So we're talking about more than just short shorts and bikinis.

And moms, while we're on the subject, here's another quick word of advice. It might be a good idea for you to check out what you wear. It's not uncommon to see middle-aged mothers wearing clothing that reveals far too much. A forty-something male friend of ours recently said, "It's amazing the kind of provocative clothing women wear these days—even at church. And I'm not talking about teenage girls here; I'm talking about their mothers! Sometimes as I walk down the halls, I have to bounce my eyes two or three times just to keep from seeing too much." What kind of message is this sending to teenage girls (not to mention the vibes men are picking up)? Moms, be a guide to modesty, not a detour around it. Teach and model modesty to your daughters.

"Modesty is something a girl is. It's a state of being; it involves how she thinks and acts. Modesty affects every part of a girl's life, from speech to dress to how she sits."[27]

JERAMY CLARK

THE SMALL-GROUP APPROACH

Perhaps the best-kept secret to talking with girls about sexuality is the small-group approach. If you're a mom, you may want to get together with others moms and brainstorm about creative and fun ways to talk with your daughters about this subject. Maybe have "ladies night out" or "girls only" parties and while munching on popcorn or doing facials, bring up the topic of dating and boys. A warm environment and group setting may help your teenage girl feel more comfortable about asking questions, or if she is shy about this, she may glean from hearing questions answered that the other girls bring up.

And Dad, you've probably already figured out that these conversations mostly fall into Mom's arena. This doesn't mean you're off the hook though, because how fathers lovingly and respectfully treat their wives should be a model of how women are to be treated. You can also point out—in general terms—how boys are negatively affected when girls' actions, dress, or demeanor negatively compound their physical and visual struggles.

~⁊~

Bottom Line: Don't just teach standards; model them.

NAVIGATING THE DATING MAZE
When Is It Okay to Date?

*Teenagers fight more battles with parents
over dating than just about any other issue.*
BARRY ST. CLAIR IN *DATING: GOING OUT IN STYLE*

I (Kent) once took a group of students to Florida for an amazing weekend retreat. You name it, we did it—riding go-carts, bodysurfing, sculpting sand. But the most unusual endeavor was our journey through a human maze. That's right, a human maze. In a football-field-sized lot, someone built a life-size labyrinth, and we spent hours navigating our way through it.

Our teens traverse through a different kind of human maze called the dating maze, and successful navigation depends a lot on our skills as guides. Here are a few practical tips that have helped us help teens:

1. *Don't wait to talk about guidelines.* First, don't wait until teenagers want to date to talk about guidelines. If you do, it's going to get nasty.

   As an alternative, lay down guidelines before kids even think about dating. As explained earlier in this book, one set of parents we know told their nine-year-old that she wasn't allowed to date until she was sixteen. When dating became an issue at fourteen, they had five years of history on their side. Sure, they were accused of being unfair, but the conflict wasn't nearly as heated as it would have been if they had just sprung the rule on her at age fourteen.

2. *Be clear.* We can't just lay down the law and be done with the

discussion. We must also clearly explain the *what, when,* and *why* behind our guidelines

The *what* are those things that constitute a date. Is a date when teens of opposite gender "officially" go somewhere, or does it include being alone together? What about double-dating—is this allowed before solo-dating? How about proms or homecomings?

The *when* is the period when dating can start. My (Kent) parents employed the age-based rule. I was allowed to double-date at fifteen and solo-date at sixteen. I (Connie) take a different approach. I encourage my girls to be friends with guys and go out in groups throughout the high school years—and save dating for college.

The *why* is the reasoning behind your guidelines. Communicating these reasons gives your kids a glimpse inside your heart. A good approach here could be to say something like: "Relationships are complicated and consume lots of energy. Yet high school is a time of personal growth and experience. It's a time to learn who you are and what you like, but it doesn't seem like getting involved in a serious relationship will help you attain this. Don't many of your friends who date end up getting so involved with each another that their entire universe revolves around one another? Aren't they missing out on all the fun? Our guidelines don't keep you from cultivating friendships with the opposite sex. They actually encourage you to get to know people and hang out with a bunch of friends. We just don't want you to rush into the dating scene."

Sharing thoughts like these shows your rules flow from a caring, not a cruel, heart.

Want another reason to encourage your teenager to hold off on dating. Check these statistics out.

Girls who start dating at age…
> twelve…91 percent lose their virginity before graduating high school.
>
> thirteen…56 percent lose their virginity before graduating high school.
>
> fourteen…53 percent lose their virginity before graduating high school.
>
> fifteen…40 percent lose their virginity before graduating high school.
>
> sixteen…20 percent lose their virginity before graduating high school.[28]

---

3. *Be flexible.* Of course, if your teen demonstrates maturity, don't just stick to guidelines that were established five years earlier as "worst case scenario" rules. As Barry St. Clair says, "Being old enough to date cannot always be determined by a person's physical age. Instead, it is an issue of maturity: spiritual, emotional, and social maturity. It shows up in the quality of relationships with parents and especially in the ability to resist physical involvement."[29] We agree!

Observe how your teen treats you, your spouse, and people in general. Look to see if he has developed personal convictions and consistently lives them out. If maturity is evident, perhaps more freedom is in order.

If, on the other hand, your teen reaches the dating age yet is immature, don't let him date. Obviously, you don't want to spring this decision on him at the last minute. Yet if you have clearly communicated that he will not be able to date once he reaches the agreed-upon age unless he acts his age, hold your ground. Maturity, not age, is what's important.

4. *Encourage group dating.* Group dating is *in* (hallelujah!). As Alex says, "I like hanging out with a bunch of friends instead of just pairing up with one girl. There are about ten of us who do everything together, and there's no pressure. We can just be ourselves." Remarkably, even when Alex started dating a girl in

the group, they continued doing stuff with the group instead of being alone all the time. He said, "It's the easiest way to keep our relationship pure." Do whatever you can to encourage this attitude! Even spring for the cost of the outing occasionally!

5. *Take the initiative.* Finally, most teens will talk about almost anything before bringing the subject of dating up to their parents. And although this book is about getting teens to talk to us, we must realize that when it comes to the subject of dating, we will almost always be the conversation initiator. At times we'll dread it (as will our teens), but if we approach each conversation wisely, it shouldn't hurt too much. Just remember the things we've discussed elsewhere: Don't interrogate, genuinely listen and care, be open to input, pay attention to timing and location (it's easier to talk over a pizza at our teen's favorite restaurant than in the car on the way to school), and talk early and often.

❧

Bottom Line: Actively guide your teen through the dating maze.

AFTER ALL IS SAID, BUT NOT DONE

A Few Extra Helpful Tips

We're almost done, but not quite. Here are a few last thoughts we'd like to share that should help bring the finishing touches to getting your teen to talk to you. Yet read ahead carefully because these may be the most challenging topics so far.

CHAPTER FORTY-SIX

PERSONALITY PLUS
Customizing Your Approach

My parents always tell me what a great personality I have.
After a while, you start to believe that you do.
ALYSSA, 15

Most parents make the mistake of shaping their conversations to fit their own personalities, instead of their teen's. This actually frustrates communication. However, knowing your teen's personality and approaching conversation in a way that will invite her to listen and share openly will foster, rather than inhibit, genuine communication.

Gary Smalley and John Trent, in their book *The Two Sides of Love*, identify four personalities and classify them in easy-to-remember terms: lion, beaver, otter, and golden retriever. Below is a brief overview of each:

Lion: Takes charge. Determined. Assertive. Firm. Enterprising. Competitive. Enjoys challenges. Bold. Purposeful. Decision maker. Leader. Goal driven. Self-Reliant. Adventurous. "Let's do it now."

Beaver: Deliberate. Controlled. Reserved. Predictable. Practical. Orderly. Factual. Discerning. Detailed. Analytical. Inquisitive. Precise. Persistent. Scheduled. "How was it done in the past?"

Otter: Takes risks. Visionary. Motivator. Energetic. Very verbal. Promoter. Avoids details. Fun-loving. Likes variety. Enjoys change. Creative. Group oriented. Mixes easily. Optimistic. "Trust me! It'll work out!"

Golden retriever: Loyal. Non-demanding. Even keel. Avoids conflict. Enjoys routine. Dislikes change. Deep relationships. Adaptable. Sympathetic. Thoughtful. Nurturing. Patient. Tolerant. Good listener. "Let's keep things the way they are."[30]

As you can see, lions are take-charge leaders. They thrive in positions of authority. They make decisions quickly. Their strength lies in being able to solve problems, but often accompanying this strength is a weakness in knowing how to relate to people. They often sacrifice people for goals.

Beavers love organization and details. They like to do things right. They get really jazzed about graphs, tables, and charts. On the flip side, they often need to work on their acceptance of people and their ability to communicate.

Fun is an otter's middle name! They're great "networkers" who can rally the troops like no one else. No doubt you'll have fun working with an otter, but make sure there's someone on the team who's actually willing to do the work…for otters often don't carry through. They like to make grand entrances and love the spotlight. Since they are people-pleasers, it's difficult for them to go against the wishes of another.

Golden Retrievers are loyal. They often absorb more emotional pain than others. They are good listeners and great encouragers, but prefer making a quieter entrance to a grander one. They, too, can sometimes have difficulties in making tough decisions. They are generally happy in nature and get along well with others.

Be Aware of Personality Types

Can you begin to see your teen's personality makeup and the conflicts that could arise between yours and hers? If you're a lion and she's an otter, you probably feel frustrated most of the time, and she feels like she can never measure up to your high expectations. If you're an otter and she's a lion, she's probably wishing you'd take life a little more seriously—especially hers.

If you have a teen that is a beaver, be careful! The last thing she needs to hear from you is, "What's wrong with you? Get a grip!" She doesn't need a swift kick in the pants—she's already kicked herself many times over. What she needs is to hear you say, "I understand that you're disappointed. Can you talk about it?" She doesn't need you to fix her problems—she needs your support.

"Lion" parents will want to fix her problem. Otters will tend to dismiss her problem too quickly, and golden retrievers may just sit back and wait for the problem to solve itself. See, all three are well-intentioned, but none will make your "beaver" child feel better.

If your teen is a golden retriever, she needs to be drawn out and given time to talk. This is especially important if you're a lion or otter—for you're apt to be happy doing all the talking. Make special effort to carve out time for retrievers, recognizing that they won't carve it out for themselves.

The "otter" teen needs to know that you like and accept her just the way she is. She thrives on attention and affection. She'll probably be your most verbal child, and if you're an otter yourself, this can result in a competition for who has the floor the most.

"Lion" teens are going to be hard workers who like to receive credit for work done. They enjoy having a sense of control (which can make life really interesting!). If you're not a lion, this can be intimidating, and if you are a lion, you may tend to constantly be vying for control. However, your goal should be to understand her, not compete with her.

Gender differences also come into play. By and large, girls tend to be more verbal than boys. Don't be surprised if your male child isn't as effusive or engaging as your female one. He may say in just a few words what your daughter will say in long, descriptive, detailed paragraphs. Keep in mind that each child is unique. Rather than comparing their gender differences or differing personalities, study and appreciate them.

Working toward deepening your understanding of your teen's basic personality and gender traits will invite more communication, about deeper issues, for the rest of your lives.

❧

Bottom Line: Understanding personality differences is often the oil that gets the hinges of communication swinging again.

CHAPTER FORTY-SEVEN

TWO! FOUR! SIX! EIGHT!

Practicing the Art of Encouragement

We kids need all the encouragement we can get.
SAM, 16

When I was a second grader, I (Connie) remember my friends and I "playing cheerleader" at recess. We knew every cheer in the high school cheerleaders' repertoire, and we could perfectly inflect every syllable. Some of my friends even had pom-poms, which greatly heightened their credibility in the eyes of those of us who didn't. Even now, in my mind's eye I can still see those red and white pom-poms flying through the air at the end of our last "rah!"

I wasn't a cheerleader when I finally got to high school, but several of my friends were. I remember how a couple of them got into a lot of trouble for talking to their boyfriends when they were supposed to be cheering. The pep club sponsor would call each cheerleader over and give her "a good talking to." Why? Because she wasn't doing her duty—she wasn't cheering for dear old Elgin High!

The sponsor would then ask the boyfriend, "Did you come to this ball game to watch the game or talk to Betsy Lou? (This always seemed like a no-brainer to me!) If you don't stop talking to Betsy Lou, I'm going to give you three demerits. Do you understand?"

The boy always seemed to get the message and would instantly head up into the bleachers, while Betsy Lou resumed cheering and the sponsor returned to patrolling her charges. You see, the pep club sponsor understood that cheerleading was a serious business. She felt the cheering could even affect the outcome of the game.

BEING OUR KIDS' MOST DEDICATED CHEERLEADER

As parents, we need to remember that cheering our own children is also serious business because our cheers have a huge impact on the end result.

Remember, you're not just any old cheerleader—you're the head cheerleader. It's your job to yell longer and louder (in a good sense!) and with greater conviction than anyone else. Even when the score seems to be 100–0 and your team (your own kids) is behind (the goals you have set for them), your cheering must rally the troops on to victory.

CHEER THROUGH TIMES OF DIFFICULTY

Your cheering tells your teen that you believe in him. This is especially important when he's going through a difficult time. It's easy to cheer a team on when it's doing well, but it takes far more effort and discipline to cheer when it has lost game after game. Your teen needs to know that you're going to cheer him on until the final buzzer has rung. He needs to know that you're proud of him, regardless of what the score looks like now.

If you don't cheer him on when the going gets tough, who will? Probably no one.

Don't ever think your efforts are in vain because he doesn't notice or appreciate your support. Actually, teens have a classic way of acting like they couldn't care less, when in fact they care a great deal. Every teen needs to know someone believes in him, and it's especially beneficial to a kid when that someone is his parent.

BALM TO A WEARY SOUL

We all get discouraged from time to time, and when we do, the power of a positive word is indescribable. Not long ago my (Connie) husband and I were doing some remodeling on a home we'd recently purchased. Various people would walk through the house when it was in its "undone" state. Some people said things like "My, this is going to be really nice when you're finished. You're going to love having a place where your kids can have their friends over." Others, though, said things like, "I can't believe you're doing this. This place is a mess. What a headache. All I can say is that I'm glad it's you and not me."

Which words were precious to our hearts? The encouraging ones, of course! Those people who had nothing but discouragement to share left us feeling yucky inside. But those dear friends who saw beyond the mess and helped us imagine the end result were like a balm to our weary souls.

CHEER, AND THEN CHEER SOME MORE

Here are some simple, easy to learn "cheers" that will encourage your teen to look beyond the mess and press on toward the goal line. A few well-chosen words may be just the balm he needs today.

- "Way to go!"
- "Wow, you really thought that through well! Your attitude is great."
- "I admire the way you do things with excellence. You handled that situation so easily."
- "You are such a blessing to me. I smile every time I think of you."
- "You're terrific! I couldn't have done it without your help!"
- "Thanks for your input—it made me see that situation differently."
- "I didn't have that much insight when I was your age."
- "You have such a wonderful sense of humor. You are so much fun to be with."
- "Thanks for sharing that with me."
- "I notice how you always go that extra mile. I so appreciate how you always see the good in people."
- "If anyone can do it, you can! I believe in you! I'm proud of you!"
- "I love you!"

Words are powerful! They have the power to pick someone up...or push his face down into the dirt. Your teen's heart will be warmed when your words of encouragement turn his face upward with hope...and heightened communication between the two of you is sure to follow.

❧

Bottom Line: Pom-poms aren't a necessity in life, but cheerleading is.

CHAPTER FORTY-EIGHT

SEIZE THE MOMENT

Seeing Life through Their Eyes

I wish my parents could remember what it's like to be young.
AIDEN, 13

⟨≈⟩

There are two memories I (Connie) have of our daughter Cassidy that still fill me with sadness. She was four years old and we were living in Tacoma, Washington. She and her twin sister filled our lives with delight, as did their newborn baby sister.

During that year, Cassidy would frequently ask if we could pack some sandwiches, go sit at a mall, and watch the people go by. Time after time she'd ask, and each time I would give her some reason why we couldn't: I had to do laundry. Or get the baby down for a nap. Or load the dishwasher. Or unload the dishwasher. Or iron Daddy's uniforms. Or make certain our house wasn't overtaken by wild kangaroos. She didn't argue or beg, but a week or two later, she'd ask again—only to hear the same kind of "no" response.

The second memory that brings me sadness is of how she would often ask if we could walk to the end of the block and sit on top of the large rock that marked the entrance into our subdivision. "Wouldn't it be fun to sit on that rock and watch the cars go by, Mommy?"

How hard would it have been for me to put the baby in the stroller and head up the hill to that rock? Not very hard at all, of course. But at the time it must have seemed monumental—for I always said, "No, not today."

At some point I realized that if I didn't want to be haunted for the rest of my life about malls and rocks, I'd better take her on these outings at least once. So one day I packed a sack lunch, and off we went to the mall. We sat on one of the benches, ate our peanut butter and jelly sandwiches, and watched the people go by. I was most likely watching the time—counting the minutes until we could leave.

On another day we walked to the end of the road, sat on the rock, and watched the cars speed by. There weren't many cars to see that day, but Cassidy didn't seem to mind. She was happy to be doing what she'd wanted to do for so long.

"Isn't this fun, Mommy?" she asked over and over again, a wide smile on her little face. And indeed it was, yet I'm not sure we ever did it a second time. I had, after all, gotten it checked off my list. I could now go back to my old ways of manning the dishwasher and keeping watch for wild kangaroos.

DON'T LET PRECIOUS MOMENTS SLIP AWAY

Younger parents are sometimes so tired and weary that they forget to look at the world through their toddler's eyes. Older parents are sometimes too tired and busy to look at it through their teenager's eyes. Wouldn't it be wonderful if we could slip on a new pair of glasses through which to see things?

There's much to be learned from seeing life through a child's eyes—regardless of the age of the child. We need to know what the "rocks and malls" are to our teens. Once we know them, we can alter our actions to say, "I value spending time with you, and if you value doing this, I value it as well."

Talk about inviting your teen to talk! This will do it. It cuts to the chase and says to your teen that you're trying your best to remember what it's like to be in his shoes. It says that you care enough to look for, seize, or create opportunities to explore the little things that delight him.

I WANT TO DO WHAT YOU WANT TO DO

One of the great things about four-year-old toddlers is that they don't remember what mom did or didn't do—at least Cassidy doesn't. But your teen will notice. As I look back on the rocks and malls, I am inspired not to let those kinds of opportunities fly by now that my girls are older. Because missed opportunities don't always come back, here are a few ways of making the most of these opportunities:

- Make a date with your teen. Let her choose what you'll do. My (Connie) girls love going to a small coffee shop near our home. They especially enjoy the mocha coffee drink that is served there. It's costly—nearly three times what a normal cup costs—so we don't get the mocha very often. But as I am writing now, I realize that the sun would probably still rise in the east and set in the west if I treated them to the mocha a little more often.
- Study your teen. What does she do when she has some spare time? Find ways of doing this with her.
- Become a sleuth! Listen for clues such as hearing her say, "There's a new movie I'd like to see," or "One of these days I'm going to try that new smoothie flavor at the bagel shop."
- Call a few of her friends and arrange for them to meet you at her favorite fast-food restaurant.
- Plan a fun evening and highlight her as the honored guest.

Our teens aren't getting any younger! Each day they're edging closer and closer to the door. Surprise them this week and offer to do something you know they really want to do. Your efforts may be met with shock, but we doubt they'll be met with much resistance! It could be that some fun conversation will ensue as well.

⋙ ˒

Bottom Line: If it's a big deal to your teen, it's a big deal!

CHAPTER FORTY-NINE

PRAISE!

Catch Your Teen Doing Something Good

*Never do I feel better than when my parents tell me they're
proud of me for something. I just wish they did it more often.*
JOSH, 15

There is something about praise that brings refreshment to a body of
any age, be it toddler, teen, or senior citizen. Praise not only makes
your teen feel great, but also has a way of generating conversation.

Today's teens frequently have pressures and stress that we didn't
experience when we were their age. As a result, we are often unaware
of the difficult times they face. However, when their lives are frequently peppered with words of praise from someone they love, it
makes their load seem a little lighter.

Here are some "praise pointers" that are sure to brighten your
teen's countenance:

- *Choose sincere words of praise, but steer clear of flattery.* Teens
  instantly recognize an attempt to "butter them up" in hopes of
  getting them to open up. Don't tell him that he handled a situation well if he didn't. Or don't tell him what a good friend he is
  to others if he frequently blows them off when something
  more interesting comes along. Instead, find something he does
  well and praise that trait. If your words ring true to him, your
  praise will be meaningful and, in turn, inspiring and uplifting.
- *Praise character.* I'll (Connie) never forget taking a psychology
  class in college. We pinned sheets of paper to the backs of each
  other's clothing, then walked around the classroom, writing
  something we liked about each person on his or her sheet of
  paper. One of the girls worked part-time in an upscale

women's store and received a large discount on her purchases there. When combined with the fact that her wealthy parents gave her a sizeable allowance each month, this all added up to a very sharply dressed gal. So it was no surprise when almost everyone wrote compliments on her paper like, "You're clothes are amazing," and "You always look so together."

When it came time to read our papers, my normally outgoing (and well-dressed) friend was quiet.

"Is anything wrong?" I asked.

"Yes," she said, "the only thing people wrote about me had to do with my clothes. I know everyone meant it as a compliment, but who wants to be known for her clothing? It's like my outside says more to them than my inside does."

Your teen is no different—he really wants to be known for what's inside, not what people see on the outside. Knowing this, praise him for something you admire about his inner person.

- *Praise motive.* Your teen may turn the basement upside down as he attempts to carve you something special out of wood for a Christmas gift. Don't dishearten him by spending just a few seconds admiring his gift because you're in a hurry to admonish him about the wood shavings you discovered on the basement floor. You wouldn't want him to think you care more about cleanliness than thoughtfulness. Look beyond the mess to the motive.

- *Praise effort.* A father was recently playing catch with his three sons. As one of the boys repeatedly missed the ball, the other two boys called out, "You missed the ball." (As if the boy didn't already know this!) The wise father, however, enthusiastically said to the boy each time, "That's great effort, son. I'm proud of you." No wonder the boy was smiling from ear to ear— Dad believed in him!

- *Praise attitude.* Is anything more admirable, more fetching, or more praiseworthy than the right attitude? In his book *Improving Your Serve,* Chuck Swindoll, a well-known speaker and author whom we greatly admire, says this about attitude:

The longer I live, the more I realize the impact of attitude on life. Attitude, to me, is more important than facts. It is more important than the past, than education, than money, than circumstances, than failures, than successes, than what other people think or say or do. It is more important than appearance, gifting, or skill. It will make or break a person, a school, a church, a company. The remarkable thing is we have a choice every day regarding the attitude we will embrace for that day. We cannot change our past…. We cannot change the fact that people will act in a certain way. We cannot change the inevitable. The only thing we can do is play on the one thing we have, and this is our attitude…. I am convinced that life is 10 percent what happens to me and 90 percent how I react to it. And so it is with you…. We are in charge of our attitudes![31]

Look for opportunities to praise your teen for having the right attitude. Keeping in mind that he won't always do things perfectly or even well, don't hold back praise until the task is completed to perfection. Because attitude is far more important than outcome, applaud a great attitude whenever it surfaces in your child.

So praise your teen. Even more, do it daily! Praising your teen tells him that you are noticing him, even in the seemingly little things that don't make big splashes. But if you let him know that his little splashes are big to you, new doors of communication are bound to open.

⟶⟶

Bottom Line: Rain praises down on your teen's parade!

CHAPTER FIFTY

ADMIT YOUR MISTAKES

The Importance of Asking for Forgiveness

When my parents admit that they're wrong,
it makes me trust them more than ever before.
JULIE, 17

～❧～

What should parents do when they goof up with their kids? Should we admit our mistakes and move on? Or would that jeopardize our position of authority and cause our kids to think we're weak? These are tough questions that every parent faces because, let's admit it, we all goof up from time to time.

Actually, *not* admitting our mistakes is a form of weakness in the scenario above. Most of the time, our kids know when we've made the wrong decision. In light of this then, our responsibility shifts to needing to model what should be done when a person makes a mistake. By taking responsibility for our actions and admitting we were wrong— and then doing all we can to remedy the situation—we provide our kids with examples of how people of strong character behave when they make mistakes.

Keeping our slate clean with our teens also keeps communication with them flowing. Offenses that have not been addressed will eventually block communication.

Not long ago I (Connie) told my daughters they could drive my car to school. After school was out, I was outside with our youngest daughter when we saw them drive by. I waved really big, expecting them to stop. They waved back and kept on driving. I was irritated and told them so when they pulled into the driveway a few minutes later: "If I let you drive my car to school, I fully expect you to blah, blah, blah…."

"Mom," they said, "we saw Jason walking up 85th Avenue by himself. His house is a long way from school, plus his brother was killed this summer in an accident, and he's had a really difficult year. We were trying to catch up with him to see if we could offer him a ride home. We didn't think you'd mind. If we stopped and talked to you, we were afraid he'd cut through a backyard and we'd lose sight of him."

"Oh…. I see."

…*Now what do I do to save face?*

CHOOSING TO APOLOGIZE

You know what I did? I apologized. I looked into their eyes, took a deep breath, and said, "Of course you did the right thing. I'm sorry I overreacted. Would you forgive me?" And, probably because they have such vast experience in this area, they forgave me right then, and the slate was once again clean.

You see, I could have instead come back at them with "It would have only taken you a second to stop and tell me what you were doing. I don't understand why you didn't do that. I could have even hopped into the car and gone with you." (Now there's a real reason to stop!)

But I was wrong—pure and simple. So a situation that could have easily escalated into something tense and chilly was instead quickly diffused when I admitted that I had been wrong.

RIGHT THE WRONG AND MOVE ON

Your teens don't expect perfection from you, but they do expect you to own up to your mistakes and try to make them right. How many times have you told them, "Do your best, and if you make a mistake, do whatever you can to make it right and then move on?" Probably hundreds.

Doesn't this motto also hold true for adults—including parents? For example, if you accuse your daughter of not putting away your sweater but then discover it lying in the backseat of your car where you left it, apologize quickly. By being quick to initiate reconciliation, you will be pointing to the fact that relationships are much more important than wounded pride.

If a fair amount of time passes before you realize you've made a mistake, make amends as soon as you realize the mistake and explain the delay.

ENCOURAGING YOUR SPOUSE

Perhaps your spouse has a problem in this area. What can you do? Lovingly talk to him. Encourage him to seek forgiveness and help him see the harm that could be caused if he doesn't. But once you've done that, your strongest means of persuading him to admit his mistakes will be the combination of your kind, gentle behavior and your prayers, and how you ask others for forgiveness. You can lead a horse to water, but you can't make him drink. But when a horse sees the other horses getting a refreshing drink from the trough—and notices how satisfied they are when they do—he will probably want that refreshment himself.

We have both learned the importance of going to God each morning and asking Him to show us any areas where we've blown it and what we need to do about the situation. It's amazing how many areas He'll actually bring to our minds!

Ask Him to help you keep your slate clean with your kids—with everybody, in fact. Do you know what will happen next? Your kids will be drawn to you. Why? Because forgiveness is magnetic...and magnetic people are refreshing to talk to.

⌐≋⌐

Bottom Line: "I'm sorry" speaks volumes.

CHAPTER FIFTY-ONE

NOW I LAY ME DOWN TO SLEEP

Making Prayer a Priority

My parents pray for me every day.
REBEKAH, 18

∽

A few years ago I (Connie) woke up in the middle of the night and discovered that I couldn't breathe. I quickly awoke Wes, who promptly ran into the kitchen and dialed 911. As he talked to the operator, he rummaged through the kitchen drawers, looking for a sharp knife in case he needed to cut a hole in my windpipe. (Did I mention that Wes is an emergency physician?) Talk about bonding!

I finally began passing a tiny bit of air—just enough to keep me from passing out...and to cause Wes to stop rummaging through the drawers. After it was determined that my throat muscles had gone into spasms to the point where no air could pass, I was placed on a muscle relaxant. However, two nights later I had another spasm and was placed on an even stronger medication. I was told there was one medication left to try if this second one didn't work. They called it "The Big Gun" because it relaxed not only your larynx muscles, but basically every other muscle in your body too. Sure enough, a few nights later I had another spasm. By this time, Wes had sharpened every knife in our house and had them strategically placed. Thankfully, though, they weren't needed.

I was prescribed "The Big Gun," and as promised, it did what the others couldn't. What a luxury uninterrupted breathing is!

"THE BIG GUN"

Did you know that there's a "Big Gun" available to you in regard to raising your teen? There is, and it's called prayer.

Prayer is simply talking to God. Yes, God! We don't have to be articulate or even know what we're trying to say in order to talk to Him. He knows what we're saying before the words leave our lips. Best of all, He understands.

Have you figured out yet that you can't do everything on your own? You don't have to! Yet we often have to discover this firsthand (sometimes many times over) before we begin tapping into God's strength and power. If you feel like you have almost reached the end of your own strength, this is a great place to be! There's Someone with far greater strength than you, and this strength is available to you. You can stop wearing yourself out and start finding refreshment in Him. He wants to be your round-the-clock Helper.

Maybe you're up against something so big that you don't know how to pray—it's as if you can't pray. There was a time in my (Connie) life when this occurred. I was experiencing great pain and heartache. I remember standing in the shower and simply calling out God's name—I knew without a doubt that He heard and understood the silent longings of my heart.

For me (Kent), I hit the prayer "wall" last year. I had let busyness and selfishness crowd God out of my life. I was making all of my own decisions, never slowing down enough to check in with Him. When I finally checked in, you know what I discovered? That He was still there!

So often we think we have to somehow "work our way up" to God. It's as if we see ourselves at the bottom of the stairs, and God at the top, and we think it's our job to figure out how to get to Him. This is craziness! Not to mention impossible! The deal is, we don't have to get up to Him—He comes down to us right where we are, just as we are.

Consider this: If you had a crying baby lying at the bottom of a staircase and you were standing at the top, there's no way you'd expect him to get to you, is there? No! You'd rush down to him, exclaiming, "Wait right there! I'm coming! I love you! Hang on!" Then you'd fly down those stairs and scoop that baby up in your arms and hug him to your chest. That, in a sense, is what God does with us. He doesn't expect us to go places we can't go. Instead, He comes to us and takes us to places we could never go on our own.

There's a wonderful promise in the Bible that states that God can do far more than we can even ask or imagine (see Ephesians 3:20). We've seen this truth lived out time and again in our own lives, and we know it can happen in yours too.

Along with all else we've stated in the book, it is imperative for you to lift your teen up in prayer. As he is bathed in prayer, you'll discover that your life is changed as well. In summation, prayer changes lives.

In addition, your teen may also be inspired to turn to God when he sees the impact seeking God has had in your life. If you're not a God-seeker, there is a good chance that your teen may see no reason to seek God either. What a privilege it is to whet a child's appetite for wanting to know God.

All the tips, all the thoughts, all the ideas we've discussed in this book point to this one summary: If you want your teen to talk to you, talk to God. As your relationship with Him deepens, your life will be filled to overflowing. And who doesn't want to talk genuinely to a person like that!

~⦿~

Bottom line: In the words of Oswald Chambers: "Prayer does not equip us for greater works—prayer is the greater work."

CHAPTER FIFTY-TWO

LETTING GO
Working Yourself out of a Job

*I think my mom's afraid that one day I'll grow up
and not need her anymore.
Just because you grow up doesn't mean
you don't need your mom anymore.*
STELLA, 16

A few years ago when my (Connie) twin daughters were entering their sophomore years in high school, they were frequently included in gatherings which were organized by kids from their youth group. Because they were our firstborns, I had no experience at letting go— and wasn't looking for any either!

My initial response was to wrack my brain trying to think of really fun things our family could do so that our girls would go out with us instead of going off with the youth group: "Who wants to eat at that new Japanese restaurant?" or "Doesn't an ice hockey game sound fun?" or "I haven't been to the zoo in years…" or "I haven't been to the moon in forever…" You get the idea! Thankfully, my husband balanced me out by encouraging the girls to go out with their friends and have a good time.

Letting go is one of the hardest things you'll ever do, yet it's crucial to your teen's development. For one thing, you're closing a chapter on your child's life…the one where she looks to you for all the answers. And it forces you to come to terms with the fact that there are certain things you simply don't have control over anymore—your older teen may choose to drink, smoke, engage in premarital sex, abuse drugs, fail her classes, or a host of other things—even though you have done (and are still doing) your best to equip her to live responsibly.

Adding fuel to the fire is the realization that your teen probably does not fully grasp the fact that the consequences of an error in judgment now (pregnancy, drinking while driving, or having drug abuse on her record) could negatively impact the course of her life forever. But even so, as your teen grows in her ability to make responsible decisions, you must overcome your apprehension and progressively let go of your control, management, and direct supervision of her activities. Why? Because when teens are held on a short rope, they usually shut their parents out altogether and rebelliously start biting at the bit to gain a little freedom.

So what is a parent to do?

TIPS FOR LETTING GO

To help you navigate this critical time in your older teen's life, here are some tips for letting go:

- Realize that when you smother, you are hindering your teen from becoming the person she was meant to become.
- Stop thinking "worst case scenario." You brought your child up to know right from wrong. Don't expend your energies on being fearful.
- When your teen makes wise decisions, shower her with praise and admiration.
- Allow her to fail. It may well be the springboard that prevents additional missteps.
- Allow her to face the natural consequences of poor judgment. Bailing her out doesn't prepare her for the real world.
- Don't tie your own self-esteem to your teen's accomplishments or failures.
- Allow her to catch a vision of who she is and who she hopes to become, not who you think she is and who you think she should become. It's great to inspire with positive words, but don't try to manipulate her by weaving personal motives into your encouragement. Instead of saying, "I admire your compassion for others—you'd make a great doctor," say something like "I admire your compassion—I can see you in a career that involves helping others."

- Realize that if you refuse to let go, anger and resentment may rise up in her and become a catalyst for her to block you out of more and more aspects of her life.
- Remember that letting go is a step-by-step process. As you see your teen exercising good judgment, reward her with additional freedoms.

The following poem, written anonymously, describes this process with great insight and clarity:

> To let go doesn't mean to stop caring;
>> It means I can't do it for someone else.
> To let go is not to cut myself off;
>> It's the realization that I can't control another.
> To let go is not to enable,
>> But to allow learning from natural consequences.
> To let go is to admit powerlessness,
>> Which means the outcome is not in my hands.
> To let go is not to try to change or blame another;
>> I can only change myself.
> To let go is not to care for,
>> But to care about.
> To let go is not to fix,
>> But to be supportive.
> To let go is not to judge,
>> But to allow another to be a human being.
> To let go is not to be in the middle arranging all the outcomes,
>> But to allow others to effect their own outcomes.
> To let go is not to be protective;
>> It is to permit another to face reality.
> To let go is not to deny,
>> But to accept.
> To let go is not to nag, scold, or argue,
>> But to search out my own shortcomings and to correct them.
> To let go is not to adjust everything to my desires,
>> But to take each day as it comes.

To let go is not to criticize and regulate anyone,
But to try to become what I dream I can be.
To let go is not to regret the past,
But to grow and live for the future.
To let go is to fear less and trust more.

One of our goals as parents is to work ourselves out of a job. This will never occur if we don't begin to let go at the appropriate time. According to countless friends who have raised children into their adult years, when teens are allowed to earn added freedom, their trust of their parents also grows progressively. And as this trust is built, they learn that they can authentically, genuinely, and openly talk with their parents. However, if teens think their parents will clamp down on them and take away all of their earned freedoms the minute they speak with them about something they are struggling with, they will quickly assume that it is not safe to talk openly with their parents.

If you have earned your child's trust because she has seen that you have been fair and have made decisions that are based on what is in her best interest—rather than your own insecurities—she will consider you a safe place where she can open her heart and seek wisdom.

You've spent years equipping your teen with wings that will one day enable her to fly. When the time comes and she's ready to spread those wings and see if they work, help her fly as high as she possibly can. Help her soar! And as she soars, remember that she's not soaring alone! The Lord goes with her, and a piece of your heart goes with her as well.

⟿

Bottom Line: Freeing your teen to soar is one of the most courageous acts you will ever perform.

IT'S NEVER TOO LATE
TO START

Alfred Nobel, the famous inventor, woke up one morning to read his own obituary in the local newspaper. It said, "Alfred Nobel, the inventor of dynamite, who died yesterday, devised a way for more people to be killed in a war than ever before, and he died a very rich man."

Actually, Nobel's older brother was the one who had died, but the experience of seeing how he would have been remembered significantly impacted Nobel. He was grieved that if he had actually been the one to have died that day, he would have been remembered for figuring out an efficient way of killing large numbers of people, and amassing a fortune while doing so.

So he initiated the Nobel Prize—the award for those whose contributions to society confer the greatest benefit on mankind. Nobel said, "Every man ought to have the chance to correct his epitaph in midstream and write a new one."

That, dear reader, is the take-away. It's never too late to start over. If you and your teen have hit a brick wall in your communication with one another, don't think it has to stay that way forever—it doesn't.

Together, you may have been down some really rocky roads in the past, and may still be on them now. Communication may even be at an all-time low in your house. Maybe there's an all-out cold war going on in your home right now. Even so, you can take heart in the fact that it's never too late to start afresh. You can also take comfort in the knowledge that as you start afresh and implement the strategies in this book, you will build healthy and warm memories together and your teen's memory of the choppy years will fade farther and farther into the background.

The possibility of starting over isn't just true for your relationship

204 *Connie Grigsby and Kent Julian*

with your teen—it's true in all relationships—unhappy marriages, estrangement between siblings, with your in-laws, and even with a parent whom you may not have spoken to for years.

We know of a father who had more or less "iced" his kids out of his life. He immersed himself in his work and showed his love to his kids by buying them things, rather than by being there for them. At first the kids enjoyed the trinkets, but over time they grew to resent their father. They even grew to resent the things that they used to think were so cool. They tried to talk to Dad—but he wouldn't listen to what they had to say. Instead, he just became defensive and accused them of being ungrateful and spoiled. After a while, they stopped saying anything to him at all.

Over a period of a few years—perhaps as a result of Mom's prayers—Dad began to feel uncomfortable with the predicament. One night he said to the family, "I've blown it. I'm sorry. Will you forgive me? Will you help me be the kind of husband and father that I should have been all along?"

Do you think they said, "Forget about it! You had your chance, but you blew it"? Absolutely not! They were thrilled! It was as if Dad had "come home." They threw their arms around him and welcomed him back! In fact, this continues to be one of their most precious "pictures" in their family scrapbook of memories.

As your own family scrapbook continues to unfold, do all you can to make sure the pages are filled with love, joy, and warm memories. If they haven't been this way so far, simply turn the page and start afresh. Time has a way of softening even the stoniest of hearts. Your job is to hang in there and be the best parent you can be.

Finally, when pages get ripped or torn—as they sometimes will—glue them back together again with love and tenderness, knowing your efforts are not in vain. If you do, one day you'll likely have an adult child look you in the eyes and say some of the most beautiful words a parent will ever hear: "Thanks, Mom and Dad, for loving me when I was unlovable. I'll never forget it."

Raising teens isn't for the fainthearted. It's a wild, exciting, and often chaotic adventure! But it's so worth it! Hang in there, and keep on keepin' on!

The Final Bottom Line: It's never too late to start over, and there's no time like the present to do so!

Thanks for reading our book!
May God bless you and your family with His peace,
His joy, His love,…and with lots of warm communication as well!

WHAT WE BELIEVE

As we wrap up this book, we'd like to share our own personal belief concerning absolute truth. We believe God, the Creator of the universe, is the Source of all truth. Even more, He is holy, perfect, all-powerful, all-knowing, just, gracious, kind, and loving. He created us to relationally connect with Him. His principles for meaningful living are found in the Bible and are designed to make this spiritual connection a reality.

In the Bible, we also discover that humanity has a significant problem when it comes to connecting with God. Sin has separated us from Him. What's more, we are so flawed that we cannot solve this separation problem on our own. We need a Savior, a Savior whose flawless life is the only thing that could pay the high penalty for sin—spiritual death and eternal separation from God.

This is where God's incredible love and grace are so clearly seen. He sent His Son, Jesus Christ, into the world. Jesus lived a perfect life and then substituted His life for ours. His death paid the price for our sins, and His resurrection defeated the penalty of sin. Through His sacrifice and victorious resurrection, our sin problem is solved, allowing us to connect with a loving God. This is what followers of Jesus call "salvation."

You might be wondering what this salvation costs.

Amazingly, it costs us nothing. That's right, nothing! Jesus paid the entire price for salvation, and He offers it to us as a free gift. If you trust Jesus and choose to follow Him today, you can experience a personal relationship with God. It's that simple.

To express such trust, all you have to do is talk with Jesus about your desire (this is called prayer). Tell Him you are sorry for your sins, ask for His forgiveness, and accept His free gift of salvation.

At times we've been asked, "How do we know Jesus and this salvation thing is real?" First of all, because the Bible says that this is so (and we believe that the Bible is God's Word!). Second, because of what He's done in our lives and in the lives of others. Once we surrendered our lives to Him, we were changed...forever.

We believe, without question, that asking Jesus to be your Savior is the absolute best decision you'll ever make. Plus, following Him every day is the absolute best way to navigate the journey of life. So, do you want to know more about salvation and following Jesus? Then pick up a Bible and read the book of John, or check out the appendix for other suggested resources.

The publisher and author would love to hear your comments about this book. *Please contact us at:*
www.multnomah.net/teentalk

SUGGESTED RESOURCES

Need more help in a particular area? Here are some resources we'd recommend on issues important to parenting teenagers.

PERSONAL DEVELOPMENT

Parents' Guide to the Spiritual Mentoring of Teens by Joe White and Jim Weidmann

SPIRITUAL ISSUES

More Than a Carpenter by Josh McDowell
Mere Christianity by C. S. Lewis
The Unknown God by Alister McGrath
Simply Jesus by Joe Stowell

MARITAL RELATIONSHIP

Love Life for Every Married Couple by Ed Wheat
How to Get Your Husband to Talk to You by Nancy Cobb and Connie Grigsby
The Politically Incorrect Wife by Nancy Cobb and Connie Grigsby
Men Are Like Waffles and Women Are like Spaghetti by Bill and Pam Farrell

RAISING TEENAGERS

Raising a Modern-Day Knight by Robert Lewis
Bringing Up Boys by James Dobson
Understanding Your Teenager by Wayne Rice and Dave Veerman
Age of Opportunity by Paul David Tripp
Parenting Teenagers for Positive Results by Jim Burns

DATING AND SEXUALITY

Finding the Love of Your Life by Neil Clark Warren

How to Know If Someone Is Worth Pursuing in Two Dates or Less by Neil Clark Warren

And the Bride Wore White by Dannah Gresh

I Gave Dating a Chance by Jeramy Clark

Dating: Going Out in Style; Sex: Desiring the Best; and *Love: Making It Last* by Barry St. Clair and Bill Jones

For Such a Time As This by Lisa Ryan

YOUTH CULTURE

The Bridger Generation by Thom S. Rainer

Understanding Today's Youth Culture by Walt Mueller

Real Teens by George Barna

1.   Wayne Rice and David Veerman, *Understanding Your Teenager* (Nashville: Word Publishing, 1999), 117–18.

2.   Ibid., 119.

3.   John Rosemond, *John Rosemond's Six-Point Plan for Raising Happy, Healthy Children* (Kansas City, Mo: Andrews McMeel Publishing, 1989), 7.

4.   Joe White and Jim Weidmann, *Parents' Guide to the Spiritual Mentoring of Teens* (Wheaton, Ill.: Tyndale House Publishers, 2001), 124–33.

5.   Robert Coles and Geoffrey Stokes, *Sex and the American Teenager* (New York: Harper & Row, 1985), n.p.

6., Mark Oestreicher, *Help! I'm a Junior High Youth Worker!* (Grand Rapids, Mich.: Zondervan Publishing House, 1996), 13.

7.   Walt Mueller, *Understanding Today's Youth Culture* (Wheaton, Ill.: Tyndale House Publishers, 1999), 157.

8.   James Sire, *The Universe Next Door* (Downers Grove, Ill.: InterVarsity Press, 1997), 16–17.

9.   Marv Penner, "Decoding the Postmodern Teenage World," *Youthworker* (November/December 2001): 55.

10.   Millard Erickson, *The Evangelical Left* (Grand Rapids, Mich.: Baker Book House, 1997), 16.

11.   James Dobson, *Parenting Isn't for Cowards* (Dallas: Word Publishers, 1987), 155.

12.   Ibid., 153.

13.   John C. Maxwell, *Developing the Leader within You* (Nashville: Thomas Nelson, Inc., 1993), 61.

14.   Dr. Gary Chapman, *The Five Love Languages of Teenagers* (Chicago: Northfield Publishing, 2001), 97.

15.   Ibid., 62.

16.   Michael Ross, *How to Speak Alien* (Kansas City, Mo.: Beacon Hill Press, 2001), 26.

17.   Philip Yancey, *What's So Amazing about Grace?* (Grand Rapids, Mich.: Zondervan Publishing House, 1997), 44–46.

18.   Stephen Klotz, "Sex in the Cafeteria: How to Handle Tough

_____

211

Sexual Issues with Your Kids," *Group,* (January/February, 2002): 37.

19.   http://www.siecus.org (accessed 12 September 2002).

20.   National Guidelines Task Force, "Guidelines for Comprehensive Sexuality Education: Kindergarten–12th Grade," *Sexuality Information and Education Council of the United States,* 1996. http://www.siecus.org/school/sex_ed/guidelines/guide0000.html (accessed 12 September 2002).

21.   Josh McDowell, *How to Help Your Child Say "No" to Sexual Pressure* (Dallas: Word Publishing, 1987), 45.

22.   Bill Jones and Barry St. Clair, *Sex: Desiring the Best* (Colorado Springs, Cook Communications Ministries, 1993), 47–48.

23.   Ibid., 101.

24.   Name withheld, "The Big M," *Youthworker* (Fall, 1994): 97.

25.   James Dobson, *Bringing Up Boys* (Wheaton, Ill.: Tyndale Publishing House, 2001), 79–80.

26.   Greg Johnson and Susie Shellenberger, *Getting Ready for the Guy-Girl Thing* (Ventura, Calif.: Regal Books, 1991), 42.

27.   Jeramy Clark, *I Gave Dating a Chance* (Colorado Springs: Waterbrook Press, 2000), 129.

28.   Bill Jones and Barry St. Clair, *Dating: Going Out in Style* (Colorado Springs, Cook Communications Ministries, 1993), 25.

29.   Ibid.

30.   Gary Smalley and John Trent, *The Two Sides of Love* (Dallas: Word Publishing, 1990), 35.

31.   Chuck Swindoll, as quoted by John C. Maxwell, *Developing the Leader within You*, 97–98.

SPEAK YOUR HUSBAND'S LANGUAGE: MALE!

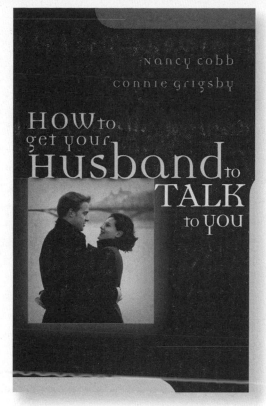

Nancy Cobb and Connie Grigsby, both popular teachers and speakers and co-authors of *The Politically Incorrect Wife* have collaborated on a primer that promises to resolve the age-old mystery of communication between the sexes—and leave men and women conversing happily. This fun, practical life-changing book will keep you alternating between laughter and tears as you discover simple ways to:

- Cultivate a sense of humor about your male and female differences.
- Open conversations with your mate, and keep them going.
- Frame what you are saying within the masculine interest areas.
- Respond proactively to what your husband shares—promoting more sharing.

ISBN 1-57673-771-3

STUCK IN UNHOLY DEADLOCK?
SO WERE WE...

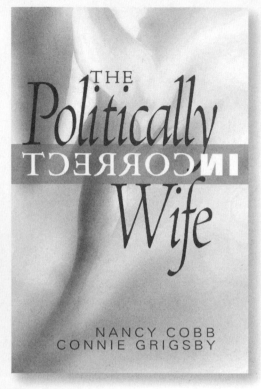

Cover Not Final

Just what is a politically incorrect wife? She's a woman who's married to her husband, not to popular culture. In relating to her man, she firmly refuses to bend to modern mindsets and strategies—like one-upmanship, tit for tat, entitlement, and "cold war"—that would ultimately damage her relationship with him.

Nancy Cobb and Connie Grigsby admit, "Our marriages were in the 'stuck' position for years until we went politically incorrect. We thought if only our husbands would change, we'd be so happy!" Sound familiar? Do you find yourself wondering, Is there more to marriage than this? There is! Get unstuck! Sidestep "marital gridlock" and start enjoying peace and warmth in your home again as you come into the joy and freedom of being a wife—God's way!

ISBN 1-59052-110-2

(Revision of *Is There a Moose in Your Marriage?* 1-57673-635-0)